Praise for *Becoming a Living Sanctuary*

"In *Becoming a Living Sanctuary*, Sandy Bowen shares her personal story of growing up as a traditional Christian and then her gradual revelation that being Christian meant more than reading the Bible and going to church. In these pages, she outlines the foundation her beliefs were built upon and the transformation she experienced as she began a personal relationship with God. Best of all, she shares advice on how you can also enjoy the benefits of becoming closer to the Father and Son through the work of the Holy Spirit."

— **Tyler R. Tichelaar, PhD and Award-Winning Author of *Narrow Lives* and *Spirit of the North***

"I am grateful to you, Pastor Sandy, for welcoming me into your heart and life in person when we were teammates doing ministry together during my years pastoring with Grace Lutheran Church in Huntington Beach. I am grateful for your invitation to everyone who reads your story, including me, to be with you in your journey of *Becoming a Living Sanctuary*. I felt loved by you. Jesus has redeemed your suffering through healing wounds and His loving presence so it has become a 'sacred wound' that gifts us with healing, love, hope, and joy."

— **Rev. Dr. Joe Johnson, Founder of *Heart of the Father Ministry***

"Sandy Bowen invites you on a unique and impactful journey in her new book, *Becoming a Living Sanctuary*. She provides an honest look into how her life was transformed by God from being just a regular churchgoer to something special. Through stories of personal growth and reflections along with prayers, readers can come to appreciate 'The Lord' even more intimately than before!"

— **Susan Friedmann, CSP, International Bestselling Author of *Riches in Niches: How to Make It BIG in a Small Market***

"In April of 2022, I took Pastor Sandy's First Alive in Christ challenge and the deep dive class that followed. I have taken every challenge and deep dive class since. Learning to listen to God's still small voice and Sandy's teachings on *Become a Living Sanctuary* have changed my broken soul into a person on fire for the Triune God (Father, Son, and Holy Spirit). The information found in this book is transformational. It shows that no matter where we come from, we all can be transformed into *a living sanctuary.*"

— **Heidi Chancey, Joyful Kingdom Living Mentee**

"Pastor Sandy and I met at a crucial point in life where I was seeking God to show me how to love unconditionally. She taught me, in action and scripture, the true meaning of God's Agape Love. Because of Pastor Sandy's teachings on God's foundation, the walls, and the roof in my life (found in *Becoming a Living Sanctuary*), He is now breaking down barrier walls from several years of pain and betrayal. Pastor Sandy exemplifies Proverbs 18:24 '…there is a friend who sticks closer than a brother.' Thank you for showing me what true love looks like!"

— **Nilka Karina, Founder of Retired Chix: Life Empowered**

"Sandy Bowen's book, *Becoming a Living Sanctuary: A Personal Journey Into an Intimate Life with Christ* uses the apt metaphor of a sanctuary to explain how she views establishing a deeply committed, lasting, and loving relationship with her Heavenly Father. Building upon a foundation of relevant scriptures from the Bible, Sandy masterfully weaves in a very authentic and touching personal journey across each season of her life in ways that demonstrate the power of her faith and the importance of passing it on to her readers. After reading this book, you will come away with a whole new understanding and appreciation for the abundant life God has in store for His children both on earth and in Heaven."

— **Mark Mears, Author of *The Purposeful Growth Revolution— 4 Ways to Grow from Leader to Legacy Builder,* Chief Growth Officer for LEAF Growth Ventures, LLC**

Becoming A Living
Sanctuary

A Personal Journey Into an
Intimate Life with Christ

SANDY MEYER BOWEN

Becoming a Living Sanctuary:
A Personal Journey Into an Intimate Life with Christ

Aviva Publishing
Lake Placid, NY
(518) 523-1320
www.AvivaPubs.com

Copyright © 2023 by Sandy Meyer Bowen

All rights reserved, including the right to reproduce this book or any portion thereof in any form whatsoever. For information, address:

Sandy Bowen
P.O. Box 5851
Mesa, Arizona 85211
joyfulkingdomliving@gmail.com
www.BecomingALivingSanctuary.com

Every attempt has been made to source all quotes properly.
All scripture references are taken from the New International Version of the Bible.

For additional copies or bulk purchases visit:

www.BecomingALivingSanctuary.com

Editors: Tyler Tichelaar and Larry Alexander, Superior Book Productions
Publishing Coach: Christine Gail
Cover Design and Interior Layout: fusioncw.com
Graphic Design: fusioncw.com
Author Photo: Brooke Preece

Cataloging-in-Publication Data is on file at the Library of Congress
Paperback ISBN: 978-1-63618-251-3

10 9 8 7 6 5 4 3 2 1
First Edition, 2023
Printed in the United States of America

Dedication

This book is dedicated to my husband, John Henry Bowen, whose love and life was transformational for me. I am grateful for our eighteen years of love and for the family we created together. Secondly, I dedicate this book to my three wonderful children, two children-in-love, and four grandsons, who have helped me carry forward love, life, and worship.

I so love you all,

Mom

Acknowledgments

My gratitude to the **Holy Spirit**, who sought me out during my time of need. You placed a hunger inside of me for more of the Lord and a greater understanding of who you are in the godhead and in our lives. My life has never been the same since my discovery of your work and presence in this world.

Reverend Dr. Brad Long and Presbyterian and Reformed Renewal Ministry, thank you for the love and many hours of teaching you have presented. I soaked it all in, and in your midst had greater confirmation of the love of Jesus and the work of the Holy Spirit. Through much of your teaching, love, and ministry, what I was experiencing was confirmed. Secondly, you were the one who, at Prayer Mountain in 1990 at Lake Castaic, spoke the prophetic message over my life to call me to ministry even when you didn't know who I was. Thank you, Brad, for your faithfulness, and for your steadfast love. My soul has much more healing because of your work and ministry along with Rev. Cindy Strickler in your teaching of Inner Healing and Deliverance Ministry. That teaching has blessed my life, and the lives of many others over the years. I so respect you and all you have done for the Presbyterian Church and others who were hungry for *more*.

Becky Tirabassi, you came into my life during a time when I needed to know how to be in committed personal prayer. My attendance at your workshop in Sacramento, California, in 1987 for the Christian

Educators organization, literally changed my life forever. Because of you, prayer became the center-post of my life, bringing forth massive transformation.

Dr. Mouw and all of my professors at Fuller Theological Seminary, I am forever grateful to you. You opened my mind to so much more than I ever knew possible. Dr. Mouw, I recall you said in the welcome address to the new students of January 1993, "I pray that Fuller will go through you, rather you just going through Fuller." Indeed, for this student, Fuller and all that was presented to me enriched my life, stretched my thinking, rounded some of my rough edges, and caused me to stretch farther than I knew possible in so many ways. Thank you for the final opportunity to share my story for the Rose Bowl Alumni gathering. The dinner, the honor, the breakfast, front row seats at the Rose Bowl parade, lunch, and tickets to the Rose Bowl game were frosting on the cake for my wonderful three years on campus in Pasadena. Thank you and blessings.

Reverend Dr. Joe Johnson and Reverend Georgie Rodiger, I honor you for your love, teaching, inspiration, and encouragement. Joe, I so appreciated working with you, praying with you, and sharing some of life in ministry with you. Thank you for introducing me to Georgie and for the incredible times we had at her home. Blessings to you. Jesus loves you, and so do I!

Reverend David Boone, you have been a continued blessing and support throughout my entire life. Even when we moved 2,000 miles away, you remained my pastor. Thank you for your love, your letters and cards, your hugs, for lunches and for your loving, listening ears. You were my pastor role model! I am sad you are no longer with us, but I do know you and Jean are rejoicing with Jesus. I love you, Dave and Jean!

Reverend Tom Naylor, you were my seminary buddy and friend along with Patsy. I have loved your support and encouragement as we have run together as the Spirit led to serve, teach, and love. Thank you, dear friend.

Reverend Phil Moran, you will be surprised by this recognition, but it is well deserved. I am so grateful for the time you spent with my children in youth ministry, and for your pure love for our family during the hardest season of our lives. Thank you for being present on the ominous day of John's death. Your presence was divinely appointed and such a help for us. Thank you for taking the lead in preparing the memorial service celebrating John's life in Jesus. Thank you for listening to me and helping me as I sorted through life without him and my new calling to serve the Lord. Bless you and Charla! Well done, good and faithful servant.

I am so grateful for all of those who have walked this journey with me in times of grief, times of growing, times of ministry, and in the writing process. There are far too many of you to mention. But I must mention my number one prayer warrior, **Chris Woodard**. You have been so faithful to have prayed for me, my family, my life journey and struggles, and this book's writing process. Bless you, dear friend. I love you dearly.

Krista Dunk, my writing coach, and **Christine Gail**, my book publishing coach, without you this book would have never been published. Krista, during the early days of COVID-19, I discovered your online book writing training. I learned a great deal from you about every aspect of writing a book and marketing it. During my time with you, I wrote two books not yet published. Those pre-books laid the groundwork for my wisdom, vision, and courage to write *Becoming a Living Sanctuary*.

Then I met Christine in early 2022 through your book publishing challenge. I knew I had something in my life that was holding me back from moving forward with publishing a book. I described that something as a "brass ceiling" over my life, preventing the progress I felt God wanted for me. During the writer's retreat, Unleash Your Rising, the "brass ceiling" was broken off, and the revelation of *Becoming a Living Sanctuary* began to spill out of me. Thank you, dear friends, for saying "yes" to helping others get their stories out. I love you both.

And finally, I want to thank other authors like **Neil Anderson**, **Richard Foster**, and so many others whose writings inspired me to open my eyes to greater truths about our Lord and His Word. Men such as **Rev. Dr. Peter Wagner** demonstrated the healing power of the Lord working through them.

All of you and so many more whose lives have impacted mine prompting the writing of this book.

Contents

Prologue ... 13
Imagine Yourself ... 15
Season 1: Laying the Foundation ... 17
    Chapter 1: Foundation of Faith ... 25
    Chapter 2: Character Foundations ... 35
    Chapter 3: Foundation of Education ... 47
    Chapter 4: Foundation of Love ... 51
Season 2: Building the Framework Securely on the Foundation ... 63
    Chapter 5: Framework of Family/Friends ... 79
    Chapter 6: Framework of Financial Preparation ... 85
    Chapter 7: Framework of Prayer ... 89
    Chapter 8: Cornerstone of My Framework Surrender ... 97
Season 3: Rooftop Reaching to the Heavenlies ... 103
    Chapter 9: Experiencing the Lord ... 107
    Chapter 10: Rooftop—The Revelation ... 115
    Chapter 11: Looking Inward and Reaching Upward ... 123
    Chapter 12: Rooftop—Spiritual Disciplines ... 131
    Chapter 13: Rooftop—Prayer as a Way of Life ... 137
    Chapter 14: Rooftop—Surrender as a Way of Life ... 143
Epilogue ... 153
Now What? ... 159
Bibliography ... 163
About the Author ... 167
Connect with Sandy ... 169

Prologue

I grew up in a family that worshiped the Lord in a traditional way. The mainline denominations in which I worshiped, served, and pastored laid a wonderful foundation for my life. The basics of a Christian life were there, yet my soul was riddled with pain, rejection, lies, and non-Christ-like ways of thinking. I so loved the Church and worship, but much of my character was broken and robbing me of a pure life in the Kingdom on Earth. I prayed the prayer, "Thy Kingdom come, thy will be done, on earth as it is in Heaven," but I never knew what that really meant.

Grateful for the foundational pieces of my life—faith, character (hard work, blending roots, and teamwork), education, and love—that were in place for me to stand on, my husband John and I began to build our life. On this foundation, we built the framework that surrounded us during the greatest crisis of our lives: his cancer battle and death. That framework was people, financial provision, and prayer. As time progressed, learning to "surrender" unto the Lord and His way became the cornerstone of the way I live.

In this book, I intermingle the stories, the concepts of my foundation, and our family framework that placed a roof over my life that would transform my home (my heart, mind, and soul) into a Living Sanctuary for the Lord to continually live in while leading and guiding my life. The journey of building this roof has been a thirty-five-year process I will share here to help you see and understand the ways of becoming intimate with the Lord, of seeking inner healing, and walking with the Lord as character develops. It is not an easy journey but one so worth the process. The Lord Jesus will be with you along the way, as will the leadership of the Holy Spirit.

I pray you will have the endurance to read this book from front to back. You may be totally surprised by the way the Lord was revealed to me, and how the Lord continues to reveal Himself, heal me, mature me, and strengthen me, for which I am forever grateful.

I have provided stopping places along the way for you to take time to ponder your life and think about how the story speaks to you and your journey. I have also provided ideas for prayer to assist you and your journey. Be blessed, be healed, and be transformed as you discover some of the Lord's ways I had never heard about.

Imagine Yourself

"Imagine yourself as a living house. God comes in to rebuild that house. At first, perhaps, you can understand what He is doing. He is getting the drains right and stopping the leaks in the roof and so on; you knew that those jobs needed doing and so you are not surprised. But presently He starts knocking the house about in a way that hurts abominably and does not seem to make any sense. What on earth is He up to? The explanation is that He is building quite a different house from the one you thought of—throwing out a new wing here, putting on an extra floor there, running up towers, making courtyards. You thought you were being made into a decent little cottage: but He is building a palace. He intends to come and live in it Himself."

— C. S. Lewis, Mere Christianity

My personal story interwoven throughout this book illustrates the dismantling of my traditional life as a Christian. The Lord rewired me, cleaned out the closets, changed the plumbing, for sure, and ensured the front door was always open to allow Christ into every thought, way, action, and decision. My house became a sanctuary for the presence of the Holy Spirit to work within me, guide me, and reveal hurts and broken ways, preparing me for Jesus' healing of every part of my life.

I wrote this book for no prideful reason, but to be the light showing you there is another way of life other than being a going-through-the-motions Christian (I did that) to a life Alive in Christ and Alive in the Spirit of God. Over thirty years, my traditional Christian life evolved into a Living Sanctuary where the Spirit of God has full freedom within to reign, bringing forth healing, clarity, revelation, and freedom as I live my life in God's Kingdom here on the earth.

Let's allow Him to lead the way!

Season 1

Laying the Foundation

"'Therefore, everyone who hears these words of mine and puts them into practice is like a wise man who built his house on the rock. The rain came down, the streams rose, and the winds blew and beat against that house; yet it did not fall, because it had its foundation on the rock. But everyone who hears these words of mine and does not put them into practice is like a foolish man who built his house on sand. The rain came down, the streams rose, and the winds blew and beat against that house, and it fell with great crash.' When Jesus had finished saying these things, the crowds were amazed at his teaching, because he taught as one who had authority, and not as their teachers of the law."

— Matthew 7:24-29

I had completed writing four chapters of this book when God revealed His blueprint for this book as the revelation of the blueprint of my life. There are three layers to this blueprint: Foundation, Framework, and Roof, which I call the Three Seasons of my book. During the writing process, The Lord, reminded me of incidents, situations, and lessons that related to each part of the residence that eventually evolved into His Sanctuary within me. When I speak about my home, my house, my sanctuary in this book, it is actually an allegory for my inner self: heart, mind, and soul.

I began as a strong house, capable of weathering many of life's storms, including the loss of my husband when my children were young (nine, eleven, and thirteen). The challenges of raising children alone and dealing with my own personal loss and pain led me to discovering the brokenness that had been within me before the loss. My foundation was there thanks to my steadfast Christian ancestors. For many generations, my family has been committed to Christ in the way they understood God. Committed they were, stiff and rigid at times, not allowing the work of the Holy Spirit and the Grace of Christ to lead the way. Nonetheless, they laid the foundation for my life.

Unraveling many parts of my life was very painful. Yet, I am so grateful for the Hound of Heaven who came to me in ways I never knew possible. Like a hound, He pursued me until He caught me and I surrendered. Then, He never let me down, even when it felt like I would drown in pain, loneliness, and the difficulties of life alone.

This first season of my life is called Foundation. It includes the following foundational pieces placed there by my family: faith in the Lord, character (blending roots, hard work, teamwork), strong commitment to education, and love. Many more pieces are within my solid foundation, but God clearly illuminated these as I was writing this book. Evidently, I stood on these as I pressed forward on my journey of becoming a Living Sanctuary.

At the end of Season One, you will have the opportunity to ponder the foundation on which you stand and think about which pieces you wish were there. (You can always work with the Lord in building or strengthening the foundation on which you stand!)

> *"Nevertheless, God's solid foundation stands firm, sealed with this inscription: 'The Lord knows those who are His,' and 'Everyone who confesses the name of the Lord must turn from wickedness.'"*
>
> — 2 Timothy 2:19

Setting the Scene

> *"For he was looking forward to the city that has foundations, whose designer and builder is God."*
>
> — Hebrews 11:10

I grew up in a Christian, suburban, middle-class home north of Detroit, Michigan, after World War II, with parents of polar opposite backgrounds. Mother grew up in the hills of Alabama near Birmingham. She was number three out of the nine children of her Southern clan. Her older sister had heart problems. Her older brother was often out doing guy things, which left Mother as the caregiver for her younger siblings. Pappaw, her daddy, was a prison guard, a low-income job in his day. Each year before school started, he traced his children's feet on a brown paper bag to get prison-issued shoes for his growing brood. Mother also learned to cook for the large family at a young age because her mother, Mammaw, was often nursing a "young'un," milking a cow, or tending to other tasks.

Daddy grew up on a farm in the thumb area of Michigan in a German-speaking family who had seven children spaced over a seventeen-year span. Daddy was the second born. He was just seventeen months younger than his older brother and two years older than his younger brother. The last four children were girls. The youngest were twins. Grandma's life as a farmer's wife was tough. She worked in the field, cooked three meals a day for her large family and the field workers, tended the garden, did all of the cooking and laundry, and cleaned the house. The three boys worked the fields from young ages. On weekdays, they did chores before school, worked in the fields after school, and when they were old enough, Grandpa hired them out to work on other farms during harvests.

Both large families kept busy trying to supply enough food to feed everyone and keep clothes on the backs of their growing children.

My parents' faith backgrounds were also quite different. Daddy's family attended Lutheran churches. The formal faith of their ancestors was a way of life for everyone. In many ways, it provided strength to the family, yet for some it was a formality. Far too often, I witnessed family attend church, singing and worshiping, then criticizing the pastor, organist, or someone in the church, undermining all of the goodness and grace of the morning.

Formal prayers were a part of our family's way of life. We prayed in unison before meals in this way: "Come Lord Jesus, be our guest, let these thy gifts to us be blessed." We all said another ritual prayer we learned at a very young age before going to bed at night. Our family's way of life followed the pattern of Sunday worship, church leadership, children in Sunday School (some attended Lutheran schools), and memorized prayers or prayers from a prayer book. Our family faith was a strength for us, as was our commitment to family. For the most part, faith and worship were an expected lifestyle for us all.

My father's family were staunch Lutherans. Everyone had to attend worship and school in German. Daddy and his six siblings attended St. John's Lutheran Church in Pigeon, Michigan, which is located in the thumb of the state's lower peninsula. Their school went from first grade to eighth grade, with one teacher, Teacher Luedtke, who was provided housing just down the street from the church and the school. Once Daddy and his siblings went to high school, they became fluent in English. Eventually, Grandma and Grandpa learned English. The love that was shown in these two families was provisional. There was never an opportunity to talk about love or one's feelings. Lots of emotions were just stuffed away, which is what I learned from a young age.

Mother's family was quite different when it came to faith. Pappaw did not attend church at all, although his mother was Episcopalian. Mammaw loved attending Springdale Baptist Church. Worship there was troubling for Mother because she didn't like the "Amens" and "Preach it, brothers" called out during sermons. When she was old enough to ride the streetcar alone, Pappaw gave her coins to ride to the big city, Birmingham, to attend the Episcopal church with her grandmother. Mother was the only one of her siblings to have this freedom. It was a true blessing for her to worship in a quieter, more meditative worship style that was more fitting to her spiritual ways. She loved spending time with Grandmother, a precious time for her because she was able to have a one-on-one relationship with this woman she treasured and who treasured her. On Sunday mornings, Mother was not caught up in the crowd of her family. The solitude and opportunity strengthened her for the mega-tasks of her week. All of the other children attended Springfield Baptist with Mammaw. As adults, some of her siblings lived the committed conservative Baptist life, while others followed Pappaw's way, not participating in church life except for funerals.

Mother's family lived in the red mud hills of Alabama, an hour's drive from Birmingham. They were a jovial bunch. Everyone attended public school; some graduated and some did not. Some were worshipers and some were not. They all gathered for Christmas Eve and Christmas Day. I am not certain how frequently they came together.

When my parents became a couple, they worked to blend their polar opposite young lives since they came from far different locations, far different worship experiences, and far different upbringings. They made commitments to unite the good things of their upbringings and faith as they understood it to be strong components of their marriage.

That was the family dynamic my parents brought into our family. Daddy was kind, gentle, and hard working. Mother was chatty, energetic, fun loving, and hard working. Although Mother was apt to say the word love, Daddy never did. My sister and I never heard words of affirmation except about our grades; therefore, I was committed to doing well in school. Feelings and emotions were never part of our communication. I clearly remember being given a sweet treat to help when I was crying rather than a kind word, a listening ear, or a hug. I developed a pattern of feeding my body when my heart was wounded, or my soul ached. This helped me learn to shove away my hurts, hiding my pain in the dark recesses of my soul. I grew up not knowing how I felt, much less how to express how I felt.

I worked hard in school, had like-minded friends, and was respected for my industrious life. The greatest pattern of love I experienced prior to marriage was in works. My parents worked hard to provide a good, clean home and yard. We had what we needed and lived in a good neighborhood. We were safe and had an organized life and home. This was my parents' way of loving us.

Love changed once I met my husband, John. He spoke of love a lot. He was a hugger and expressed his love to me, our children, and others. This dramatic difference changed me, building my foundation of love more completely and tenderly. I will write about that in Chapter 4. I am so grateful for the growing understanding of tender love and sacrifice of self for others he helped me to find.

Dedication to my studies earned praise from my mother, creating a way of life in which I sought love through works. Studying, isolation, and shyness became the rhythm of my life. My emotions were stuffed deep within me just like they were for my father and his family. My sister grew up spunky and enjoyed being the center of attention. She took tap dance lessons and happily tapped away with Mother in the kitchen as they practiced, slap-step-step, slap-step-step, left foot, slap-step-step, slap-step-step. I, on the other hand, was tucked away in my bedroom practicing the accordion. I was jealous of the two of them practicing together in the kitchen while I obediently practiced the accordion isolated in my bedroom. Yet, sitting alone and working away suited me. The opportunity to participate in an activity like tap dancing might have brought me out of my hiding place and introduced me to a more active and energetic life.

My family and John built a solid foundation for my life and my children's lives, which helped us through the major loss we would experience; we had growing faith. I worked hard, blended lifestyles well, and understood teamwork. I am grateful for the solid education and career I earned, and the depth of love that has been expressed in so many ways throughout my life. This first season of this book unfolds each of these areas of my life, begun by my parents and then strengthened by John and me during our eighteen years of marriage.

Reflection Time

Pause to think about yourself as a child.
What is your life built upon that gave you a strong foundation?

_____
_____
_____

Did you build on faith, education, hard work, love, or something else?

_____
_____
_____

Is your family similar on both sides? If not, how are they different?

_____
_____
_____

Are the differences a challenge for the peace of your family dynamics?

_____
_____
_____

Prayer Time

Pray for your family and your family dynamics. Pray for peace and unity, grace and love.

Chapter 1

Foundation of Faith

*"By **faith** Abel brought God a better offering than Cain did. By **faith** he was commended as righteous, when God spoke well of his offerings. And by **faith** Abel still speaks, even though he is dead. By **faith** Enoch was taken from this life so that he did not experience death: 'He could not be found, because God had taken him away.' For before he was taken, he was commended as one who pleased God. And without **faith** it is impossible to please God, because anyone who comes to Him must believe that He exists and that He rewards those who earnestly seek Him. By **faith** Noah, when warned about things not yet seen, in holy fear built an ark to save his family. By his **faith** he condemned the world and became heir of the righteous that is in keeping with **faith**."*

— Hebrews 11:4-7

I sat alone in our bedroom on the evening of June 20, 1987, my world closing in around me, emptiness and devastation engulfing my soul after laying John, the love of my life, to rest. I couldn't cry. I couldn't really feel. I just sat staring at the ceiling more exhausted than I had ever been before. For three years I had held it together as my loving husband's body failed him and, ultimately, our family. On that devastating night, my children were in bed, my parents and sister were resting downstairs, and I was alone—more alone than I had ever been.

All I could do was feel my heart beating, listen to my shallow breathing, and stare at nothing. The emptiness was overwhelming. Exhaustion was rocking me to sleep to comfort my weary soul. I slept soundly and deeply that night and awoke with a gasping prayer, "Now what, God? Now what? How do I do this alone? Soon my family will return to their homes in Michigan and Florida, and I have to carry on with our now family of four. How can I be mother and father, teacher and home manager? How will I handle the cars, the house, the yard, the children's faith, my students, and all that life has for us without someone to share all of life's decisions, challenges, and joys with?" Finally, I drifted off into an exhausted deep sleep.

Soon, I heard movement in the house. Everything I was dealing with had to be tabled while I attended to a house full of family. Mother, Daddy, my sister, and her son would be with us for another week. That was good in some ways, but it also meant I would have to walk through those days with this huge aching gap in my soul while playing host to my extended family. Over breakfast, decisions were made to travel to some fun locations in our Northern California area. Daddy would do some repairs around the house, Mother would help get the house in order, and my sister would have fun with her nieces, nephew, and her son. And I would be present and thankful for their presence, yet longing to just be alone with my grief.

Our trip to San Francisco and Alcatraz Island was a helpful distraction, but I inevitably felt John's absence, constantly turning to share a moment with him only to find him gone. San Francisco was his favorite location for us to visit as a family; we had visited it many times during our four years of California life. Everywhere I looked, memories rushed through my thoughts that day: the times of joy, the times of celebration, and the times of his sharing his childhood memories in San Francisco, including Fisherman's Grotto #9, Crab Louie salads, Pier #39, clam chowder in a bread bowl, the smell of ocean air, the seals lingering at Seal Rock, Lombard Street, the trolley rides, penny arcades, Chinatown, Coit Tower, Ghirardelli Square, deep sea fishing, chocolate-covered gummi bears, and all the stories of his past. The day was helpful and painful all in one.

Other fun activities filled some of our time that week. We tried to be a family enjoying California life on the beach and the tourist attractions…but the pain lingered as the week flew by.

Then it was time for my family to leave. Daddy had repaired door hinges, fixed small appliances, and performed many other tasks. With the house in order, we dropped my family off at the airport, hugging them goodbye for now and returning to our home and our drastically different new life. I was grateful for their presence and all they had helped us with, yet I couldn't help focusing on what life would look like without my love, the center of our family.

The days that followed were filled with conversations with friends and trying to develop some form of normalcy. Fortunately, the children had summer camp to look forward to at the end of June, and I would have some time to rest in my sorrow alone, sleeping in if I needed to, crying, praying, and figuring out how to create our new home. My first choice was to redo *our* bedroom into *my* bedroom.

John's friend Larry, who had come to visit him every day on the way to his afternoon shift, stopped to see how he might help me. I agreed I would need his strength to rearrange the furniture in the master bedroom and paint the walls. Larry was truly a blessing, and the major work was completed in a few days. I packed up all the old bedding and bought new, feminine sheets and a comforter. Another friend gave me a body pillow to help me feel as if I had a companion at night. I replaced the pictures on the walls, creating a spa feeling in which to pray and seek God.

Once everything was in order, I began to stand more firmly on the foundation of faith my family had given me forty years earlier at a time when they had no idea how I would need to hold on so tightly to this basic faith in Jesus, prayer, and worship.

The Impact on Our Future

> *"Start children off on the way they should go,*
> *and even when they are old they will not turn from it."*
> — Proverbs 22:6

In the following days, weeks, and months, good memories and difficult memories came swiftly to the surface as I searched for a way to live without my best friend and lover. My father's family, staunch Lutherans with firm German heritage, had dutifully poured faith into all of our lives. My great-grandparents on both sides of my dad's family had come to the United States for a new life, a free life, and to become successful in a new land. My grandmother's grandfather brought his entire family to America from Germany in the mid-1800s purely for religious freedom. He had such a strong commitment to the Lord to uproot the family—ten children—while he was in his sixties for the sake of his authentic faith in Jesus Christ, our Lord and Savior. In the next generation, my grandpa's parents moved their family to Michigan for a more fruitful life and to join the adventure of his brother in farming and marketing. Their faith was deeply rooted in Christ.

The two Meyer brothers' wives felt that German was the only language right for worshiping God, so when the church wanted to incorporate English into the service, they refused to attend services and worshiped in their parlor in German. One of my dad's cousins told the story passed down to him that these women believed people who worshiped in English were going to Hell, and they would have no part of this blasphemous worship. A bit legalistic we would say, but it paints a picture of the serious commitment to the church, God, and worship this family stands on.

That is the family heritage I reflected on during my nighttime tears, prayers, and processing. Faith in God was central to our family, belief in Jesus as Lord and Savior was spoken of and sung about, and being part of a church was a way of life. Yet that heritage was not giving me comfort in this tragic time. My family went home, leaving me to fend for myself. The rest of my family in Michigan talked about us Californians, but none of them reached out to help or talk. I was left alone with my children to pioneer a new way of life.

My family's heritage gave us a foundation to stand on in this tragic time. Blessed readers, if you don't have a family heritage of participating in a faith community, find someone who can help you find one. When we met, one thing John loved was my family's faith. He grew up in a military family, moving from base to base, with little exposure to church. John told me the neighbors took him and his brother to church on Sundays, or he rode a church bus to a local church. Every new base brought a new situation. But people and churches went out of their way to get John and his brother to church, for which I am grateful.

John had some faith within him, so when he met me, he wanted more of what he had tasted. On our second date, we went to church together and had lunch afterward. We did that every Sunday after.

In my family, everyone married another Lutheran. That was the way life was lived. I didn't do that, but as soon as we were married, John wanted to take adult confirmation and become a Lutheran. We attended membership classes together, and when he became a member, I joined also with a transfer of membership from my former congregation. That way, our life as a married couple was grounded in the faith of my heritage, and all was well. We prayed the table prayers, went to church, and gave some money to the church.

Church was a central part of my life, but it was not enough when life took its terrible twists and turns. Just going to church, reciting rote prayers, and talking about God was not enough for me in those dark nights of the soul. Nor was it enough for John as his body began to crumble. We had fit God into the nooks and crannies of our lives, but we lived as the world lived in so many ways. God was the base, but not as much a way of life as God desired. He was worshiped in a formulated Lutheran way, but I never knew Jesus personally. In fact, I never knew that Jesus wanted that kind of relationship with me/us. Were we in for a surprising revelation!

Before John's health crisis, we moved through tough times by continuing to attend church, praying before meals, and teaching our children the Bible stories. We took them to church, Sunday School, and Vacation Bible School. For several summers, our family, along with nine or ten other church families, attended family camp for a week where we developed wonderful friendships. Our memories became a part of our hearts, uniting us with those families forever. In fact, several of the teenagers became our exclusive babysitters. We had potlucks and New Year's Eve parties, and some of us golfed and played racquetball. We worshiped or took classes during the Lenten Season and attended most events at our church, but something was seriously missing when this crisis arose.

My heritage, our church friends, youth group, Bible studies, and all of our fellowship friends didn't completely carry me through this dark time. I knew there was something more I hadn't experienced or been taught. I must say right here, I am so grateful for the foundation of my heritage, for our friends and churches in our town of Vacaville, California. Without them we would have been so lost, but with them, I still didn't know how to move forward. I didn't know what to do about the biggest, darkest pain ever.

Building a Foundation of Faith

> *"For no one can lay any foundation other than the one already laid, which is Jesus Christ."*
>
> — 1 Corinthians 3:11

With our family faith heritage, church as a place to go on Sundays, and for events throughout the week, we could move forward. That we did. So, I must say, build the foundation if you don't have one. Find a church body where you can learn and grow with people who care about you and your family.

Reading multiple Christian books was part of my strength during John's final year. Along with reading a chapter of the Bible, it brought me peace each night before I laid my head down to rest. A year's worth of teachings by a broad spectrum of authors expanded my foundation, especially on the work and power of the Holy Spirit.

Without the foundation I stood on, I don't know how I would have handled this trying time. As it was, I developed an insatiable appetite for more of God, more of Jesus, and more of the Holy Spirit. Thank goodness my foundation meant I was better able to discover the presence of God in my life, which helped guide me and helped me walk through the muck and mire of life during John's last year and into the future.

Just as I had a faith foundation, John and I made the commitment from the beginning that our family would be rooted and grounded on the faith of my forebears, so our children would have a foundation to stand on as they stepped into their futures. And fortunately, that foundation was strong enough that they are now providing a similar foundation for their children in even better ways than John and I ever knew how to do. Praise God! I believe during this crisis and in the days and years after, with the help of the Lord, I helped my children build a stronger understanding of faith, love, and service. Now I watch that intentional teaching reflected in such precious ways as my grandsons grow, worship, and serve the Lord.

In God's perfect plan we are able to follow the faith heritage of Jesus back to Abraham when God promised him a nation as large as the number of stars in the sky. From Abraham to Jesus, there were thousands of descendants, yet only a few were mentioned, just as there are a few who stand out in my family heritage. Those few followed the faith of our ancestors. Some are pastors, church musicians, Christian school teachers, church leaders, and Sunday School teachers. Many of the others are still part of the clan, and most of them are Christ worshipers. So it was in Abraham's tribe; some were leaders of the faith, others were warriors, and some were grafted into the Israelite tribe. God knew the hearts of the faithful who passed on the faith to their children on and on down the line. As I look back as far as I am able, our family was blessed with committed servants who taught their children, and so it continues with many of us, including my children and my children's children.

Reflection Time

Write about your faith and its foundations. Did it begin generations ago, or are you creating a faith path forward for you and your loved ones? How are you intentional about living your faith?

_____
_____
_____

How has your faith assisted you with life's challenges?

_____
_____
_____

How has your faith helped you find friends you can trust to walk with you on God's path?

_____
_____
_____

Prayer Time

Thank God for your faith journey and talk with Him about how you want it to progress in His ways.

Chapter 2
Character Foundations

> *"Whoever walks in integrity walks securely,*
> *but he who makes his ways crooked will be found out."*
> — Proverbs 10:9

Since I grew up in a family of faith, we learned to live by many of the Bible's truths. I am not going to lie and say we were perfect by any means, but a faith foundation led to a balanced home. My parents seemed to seamlessly blend their very different roots into our family life; each had family responsibilities, and they were faithful to those responsibilities, which created teamwork, and they both worked hard. This section will elaborate more on those areas of our family's character that have spilled out from my parents to me as the parent of my family and now into the families of my children. I would say good roots were placed in this family's character, which is evident in my children and grandchildren. You may have other character traits that stand out for your family. I will challenge you later to explore your family character or your own personal character.

Blending Roots

> *"Then He called the crowd to Him along with the disciples and said:*
> *'Whoever wants to be my disciple must deny themselves*
> *and take up their cross and follow me.'"*
> — Mark 8:34

My parents not only came from very diverse faiths, but their cultures and where they grew up were equally diverse. Mother grew up in Tarrant City, Alabama, in the 1930s. As one of the older children, she was required to carry a lot of the load in caring for her family and their home. She loved her parents and siblings, yet she held a grudge about all of the responsibility she had to carry as a young girl. I imagine it was very appealing for her when she met Daddy while she was still in high school. He was a handsome Army sergeant from Michigan who was stationed at Camp McClellan, Anniston, Alabama. Mother's best friend was dating one of Daddy's Army buddies, so they were introduced through these friends and the match was made. Mother was pretty and fun loving; she loved to laugh and dance. I am certain that was appealing to a farm boy who was in the big city preparing for his deployment to Germany during World War II.

The dichotomy of my parents' family backgrounds caused quite the diversity in our upbringing. Mother's family was backward and mostly uneducated, still living in the after-throes of the Civil War. Daddy's family were German immigrants, which made life difficult during World War II since America was fighting Hitler's regime. Daddy once told me how difficult it was for him to be an American soldier in Germany, the home of his ancestors, and to see the dead civilians laying all around. Women during Hitler's era were given badges according to the number of children they had given birth to in order to encourage the growth of the Aryan race. It broke his heart to see women wearing their badges of honor lying dead on the ground.

As I reflect back, I see how my Southern mother chose to fit into the culture of the North where my dad was from. She desired to move from her birth location to start life again in her way. When I was growing up, we would have family gatherings for summertime picnics, weddings, confirmations, baptisms, and funerals. As the family gathered, I never thought about who my dad's siblings were, or who married into the family. Everyone was just family to us kids. I did know who my father's parents were and my mother's mother because they were located in far different states, but within each family, the adults all just blended together for us kids. On my mother's side, Daddy just fit in with all of my uncles. They went hunting and were silly in Mammaw's backyard together as they lit firecrackers and joked with each other.

An uncle was an uncle; it didn't matter if he were a blood relative or an in-law relative. This was on both sides of the family. Everyone appeared to get along, and no one stood out to us kids as an out-law. I believe this helped my parents blend their different backgrounds. My father's family's faith consumed his life, and Mother just stepped into it. In my parents' generation, men had men's chores and women had women's chores. They seemed to willingly do their part. Yet my parents were never outspoken about chores. I never heard either of them say, "I won't do that because it is a woman's chore or a man's chore." In fact, they both worked in the yard and around the pool. They worked together on big projects like painting and remodeling the basement. Here, too, the ways of working in a family were blended, making it natural for me to learn to blend life in our marriage.

From the beginning, John and I talked a lot about our childhoods and what important elements we would carry forward into our family. For example, I learned to eat foods from my husband's California and world perspective, and he enjoyed the German-American cuisine he encountered, especially in family gatherings. My family received my husband just like we received the spouses of all of my cousins. We all had equal footing in my family of origin. We were determined to share the care of our home and the raising of our children. Faith would be a centerfold of our life. And we truly enjoyed celebrating birthdays and holidays with my family and fun occasions with our friends.

I know this acceptance does not happen in a lot of families, so I feel blessed this was a strength passed on to our generation. We joyfully have shared many holidays with my two married children's in-laws, and I am good friends with them. This brings peace to our family and a joyful anticipation of gathering together.

One character strength for our family is working together on common goals and finding a happy medium to live in peace. I, too, married someone who was from a very different background. We melded our lives together in a far different way than my parents had, but we willingly worked things out as a team. My faith also was all-consuming for my way of life, and my husband joyfully stepped into our faith, joining the Lutheran Church soon after we were married. So often, blending life, family, and ways means dying to self in order to be willing to shift ways and ideas. It takes flexibility, love, and a will to want to live a life united in the ways of life.

Reflection Time

Is blending your ways an easy character trait for you and/or your family?
_____
_____
_____

How have you been able to do that in your home, work, or neighborhood?
_____
_____
_____

Have you thought much about dying to yourself for the good of a relationship?
_____
_____
_____

Prayer Time

Pray for preserving your family heritage and what you will be intentional in carrying forward in your lives. What does God want you to see that pleases Him?

Hard Work

> *"Whatever you do, work at it with all your heart, as working for the Lord, not for human masters, since you know that you will receive an inheritance from the Lord as a reward. It is the Lord Christ you are serving."*
>
> — Colossians 3:23-24

Daddy's hard work on the farm and his commitment to basketball and finishing his high school education all played a part in his future. Once he graduated, he worked on many local farms and was well known for his hard work and dedication. One day, a recruiter from Michigan Bell Telephone Company came to our rural area of Michigan looking to hire young farmers to work as linemen. Several farmers mentioned my father's name. When the recruiter and Daddy met, he offered Daddy a job…but he had to be twenty-one before he could be hired. Climbing telephone poles was difficult and dangerous, so one had to be a legal adult. As soon at Daddy turned twenty-one, he was hired. What an exciting day that was. The job gave him the freedom to make a good future.

Often, Daddy worked out of town because many more telephone lines were being installed in the thumb area of lower Michigan. His work and travel allowed him to purchase his own car, and he was admired in his small town.

As Michigan phone lines were expanding, so was the need for linemen on the frontlines in Germany for the war effort. Finally, Daddy was eligible for the draft. Farmers were often exempt from the draft.

Daddy had very flat feet, so he failed the medical exam. He couldn't march, but his knowledge of communication technology opened the door for him to enter the Army as a sergeant—which led to a higher rank, higher pay, and a great deal of prestige.

When Mother and Daddy married, his work ethic and her experience as a caregiver and housekeeper came together in a special way. I am sure there were some hard adjustments for them in the beginning since they married in Michigan and stayed a short time before moving to Atlanta for training, and then he was deployed to Europe on a large military transport ship. Mother returned to Alabama to finish high school and work in a department store as she waited for her handsome soldier to return. While Daddy was deployed—a year and a half—they exchanged many love letters!

Fortunately, Daddy's job in the military laying telegraph lines for the commanding officers to communicate kept him away from battles and killing others, yet the evidence was all around him and truly heart breaking.

When the war was over, Daddy returned to Alabama to pick up his bride and travel back to Michigan on a bus. By that time, his family had moved to Utica, Michigan. They rented a small home in the downtown area, and Daddy returned to his job with Michigan Bell.

Daddy's work ethic earned him several promotions and raises, and soon my parents bought a home about thirty minutes away from the family.

"Commit your work to the Lord, and your plans will be established."
— Proverbs 16:3

Sometimes, John and I told our children, "Make hay while the sun shines." Which meant work hard when it is time to work so we all can go do something fun. With that attitude, our children learned to help around the house at young ages. I was so grateful for that because later, when tragedy struck, the four of us became a solid team tending to the household chores and homework so they could play sports, be in Girl Scouts, and participate in youth group.

Actually, I thought working hard was the only way to live. I embraced my parents' work ethic in my schoolwork, in caring for my bedroom, and by helping in the yard. My dedication opened many doors for me and helped me change many situations where God placed me—in chaotic classrooms, my hard work brought peace and success; in churches, I worked hard to bring order to chaos in storage rooms, programs, and the governance structures; in ministries, I helped organize financial structures, warehousing donations, and running the ministry.

Hard work leads to organization, order, and peace.

Reflection Time

Was hard work a part of your family's way of life?

_____
_____
_____

If so, have you carried that forward? If not, how have you dealt with that?

_____
_____
_____

Hard work is part of living a disciplined life. What in your life has been encased in discipline?

_____
_____
_____

How are/were your children or grandchildren raised regarding chores and responsibilities?

_____

_____

_____

Prayer Time

Pray about your family and personal life. Is hard work an integral part of the way you live? What do you think the Lord is saying to you about your work ethic? Listen and pray about this. Has your hard work brought you favor?

Teamwork

> *"Two are better than one, because they have a good return for their labor: If either of them falls down, one can help the other up. But pity anyone who falls and has no one to help them up."*
>
> — Ecclesiastes 4:9-10

Working hard and molding our very different family backgrounds together was part of the early years of our marriage. John was ten years older than me. When we started out, I was starting my career as a teacher, and he was already established as a quarter scale draftsman at the General Motors Technical Center in Warren, Michigan. I worked hard in my first few years of teaching, trying to be the best teacher I could be while we worked on a fixer upper home. Within the first year, we bought a former farmhouse and turned it into a nice family home. Teamwork was at the heart of our family. Working together was one of the strengths of our marriage. John was not afraid to change a diaper, feed a child, prepare a meal, or fold a basket of clean clothes.

In fact, one day John's mom, whom I call Mom, was visiting from California. She and I loved going to the fabric store together to pick out some patterns and material for her sewing projects. Each year when she came to visit, she made something new for us since she was a seamstress/tailor by trade. One Saturday, Mom and I were gone a long time. We had a lot of fun. As we walked into the back door, we found John with everything out of the refrigerator; he was cleaning it and defrosting the freezer. It was such a special gift to me.

And I would take John's many shoes out of his closet while he was at work and use paste polish to make them clean and shiny. We were a hard-working team who also loved to play and go on outings. The model was work hard and play hard. We instilled this in our children as they grew up.

From an early age, our children were taught to participate in maintaining our home. They were, of course, taught to clean up their toys before Daddy came home from work so the house was not chaotic when he returned, and we could all enjoy the evening activities and fun. It was a family rhythm. Daddy would be home at 5:30 p.m., so a little before that, we started singing, "Clean up, clean up, everybody clean up." The children would scurry around finding all of the toys in the family room and placing them in their toy box. Of course, I worked with them because we were teaching teamwork.

When the children reached school age, I taught them how to set the table for dinner. Once they were all old enough, they took turns setting the silverware, and I set out the dishes and glasses. Next, they learned to clean off the dirty dishes and place them on the counter. One would set the table; one would clean off the dishes. The next stage was to learn how to rinse off the dishes and load the dishwasher.

Household chores like putting away their own clean clothes, folding clothes, and taking their dirty clothes to the laundry room on wash day made them a part of caring for their attire. Later, they each had their own bedroom and were responsible for keeping it orderly as part of the team effort needed in having an orderly house.

Dedication, hard work, and knowing how to tend to household chores helped my children as they grew and needed side work to help get through school. Cleaning others' homes, tending to church ladies' yards, and cutting neighbors' grass brought in much needed money as they grew. That work ethic was the strength of our family once we were a foursome, and it continues to play out in our children's adult lives and now their children's lives. It pleases me to see my grandsons get up on Saturday mornings with their list of chores to complete so they can have a fun day.

The blessings of our family's foundation have been beneficial for a hundred years, from the years on the farm to a family looking to move forward during and after a major tragedy, to the next generation of four grandsons and the fruit they will bring forth in the world.

Reflection Time

Have you created a teamwork setting in your home? If so, what does it look like? If not, why not?

_____
_____
_____

What was your family like when you were growing up regarding chores and order? Write about your family's way of handling household chores.

_____
_____
_____

Did you work as a team? What was it like?

_____
_____
_____

Are you a team player? Are you the leader or a follower? What does it look like for you?

_____
_____
_____

Character Reflections

Character is a part of you that is trustworthy and reflects godly ways of living and being in your family, in your neighborhood, at work, or at play. Examples: trustworthy, caring, dependable, hard-working, team player, positive, etc.

Each person has character traits that are their strengths. What are yours?

_____
_____
_____

Prayer Time

Pray about your home, work, and/or business situation. Do those involved function as a team? Does God want you to change something? Ask Him.

Chapter 3

Foundation of Education

> *"I said to myself, 'Look, I have increased in wisdom more than anyone who has ruled over Jerusalem before me; I have experience much of wisdom and knowledge.'"*
>
> — Ecclesiastes 1:16

My paternal grandpa's three boys were very valuable on the farm and in the local community. They had chores to do before and after school, and during the summer, Grandpa hired them out to local farmers for extra family income. Daddy worked hard yet played basketball in high school and insisted on completing his education. Grandpa wanted Daddy to drop out of high school to work fulltime. Daddy refused. He was the first in his family to graduate with a high school diploma. Then the rest of his younger siblings followed in his footsteps. Once Daddy was out of high school, he worked on other farms and their own until he got his job at Michigan Bell.

Mother also thought it was important to earn her high school diploma. After they were married and Daddy went off to war, she returned to Tarrant City, Alabama, to complete her high school education. They were married in November. She had stepped out of school her senior year and returned to finish once he was deployed. Mother and Daddy were proud of their diplomas, and they wanted even more for my sister and me.

I was the oldest and an introvert. Working hard at school was as natural for me as working hard at Michigan Bell was for my dad and working around the house was for my mother. I didn't know of any other way than to do my job well. I was never the smartest kid in the class, but I made up for that by working hard and always completing my assignments. I loved books, and Mother invested in a new Golden Book for me each week. That love for books has never left me.

When I was about three, Mother took a most treasured picture of me standing next to Daddy as he read a book to me. Looking at that scene makes my heart smile because it reveals an intimate moment my father and I shared. I still think about it and continue to treasure it. Reading opens up the world in so many ways, and it certainly did for me even at that early age.

My desire to read, study, and work hard took me to Michigan State University. I got in easily because in high school I had good grades and I was an officer in several clubs, a member of the synchronized swimming team, and a member of National Honor Society. My drive to be educated helped me when my studies were overwhelming. I would never give up. After two years of basic classes, I made it to the safety of the College of Education, where I flourished.

My degree opened the door for me to get my first position as a full-time teacher immediately after college. To earn a permanent teacher's certificate in Michigan, I was required to take a hundred units of additional coursework to strengthen my teaching abilities. Those units, which I took one by one after each day's work, quickly added up, allowing me to use them toward a master's degree in elementary education when my youngest was an infant. The master's program was important for my soul since I was home with three pre-school children. I needed some adult stimulation. And for a lifelong learner, this was the catalyst that carried me through diapers, formulas, naps, laundry, cleaning, and cooking. Studying hard grounded me in my effort to help make a better life for our family.

John's family was very different from mine. His father's military career afforded them great opportunities to live in Germany and several locations along the West Coast. The transient military life became more difficult when John was a junior in high school and active in sports. John wanted to stay in Antioch, California, where he felt at home, to finish high school. One of his coaches offered to let John live with him, but John's father refused to allow him to stay behind. In response, John quit school and joined the Navy. He was not yet eighteen, so his mother signed the papers, which allowed him the opportunity to become a sailor at age seventeen.

John took classes while in the Navy, and he was always learning something to help him get a new job or a promotion. And he earned a GED along the way.

Since I was a dedicated learner and teacher, I took the lead on our children's education to ensure they worked hard in school and did well. They had to complete their homework. I helped them prepare for tests and projects, and I did whatever it took for them to learn and be prepared for the future. My daughters earned bachelor's degrees and one has a master's degree. My son has an associate's degree in computer aided drafting, which has helped him in the construction business. And now, my grandsons are being taught the importance of education, whether it is a trade school, a Bible college, or a mainstream college.

Working hard, studying, preparing, and helping around the house are parts of our family's rhythm of life that flows onward. My children and grandchildren balance education, sports, the beach, worship, and service to others in a wonderfully healthy way. It delights my heart to see that dedication being passed along generational lines, carrying forward the ethic of hard work, love of God, and having fun.

Reflection Time

Do you have a foundation of education? This might not mean a degree, but have you been a lifelong learner in other ways?

What have you been passionate about learning? Is it part of your life's foundation?

How have you carried forward the pattern of learning in your family? Are books, courses, workshops, conferences, retreats, or other means of learning an important part of your life?

Prayer Time

Pray about your life regarding learning. Thank God for all of your teachers, courses, and books. Ask Him how you should proceed with learning for the rest of your life.

Chapter 4

Foundation of Love

"Dear friends, let us love one another, for love comes from God. Everyone who loves has been born of God and knows God."

— 1 John 4:7

Healing a Parched Soul with Authentic Love

Love looks very different to everyone. The way we love is influenced by our family, the people who raised us, how it plays out in our marriage or friendships, and by our personal love languages. I grew up in a family where providing for us and teaching us about hard work were the way we were loved. Mother did hug us and tell us she loved us, but Daddy was the quiet one, never expressing much love until I was in my fifties. In fact, when he wrote, "I love you," in a card he sent me, I wept as I stared at those important words. They were like rain on the parched soil of my soul. He often signed cards, "Love, Daddy," but my emotional response was nothing like it was when I read the words, "I love you." The "I" and the "you" landed so intimately and deeply in my empty soul. I desperately needed to hear and feel those words I had waited to hear for fifty-five years.

Since my own family lived in California, we saw my parents infrequently. We always hugged when we came together, but it felt like a perfunctory action. It didn't land deep in my soul. My lonely, crying heart became evident during my inner healing journey. As I listened to my heart, I discovered I had not bonded with Mother as a newborn for some reason, so no matter what she did or said, our connection didn't seem real. On the other hand, I had somehow connected with Daddy, and I felt like I was Daddy's girl until my sister became a toddler and was fun and outgoing. Then I felt pushed aside and retreated deeper into myself, my hunger for love continuing to fester. I substituted accolades for good grades, leadership roles in clubs, and comments about my good behavior for the deep feelings of authentic love.

Our family would never talk about our feelings when I was growing up. My parents probably never had that privilege when they were young either, so I am not faulting them by any means. Talking about feelings was just not part of our lives. We lived a good, middle-class life, working hard, going to church, eating well, and enjoying a relatively peaceful home, but we did not show depth of emotion, love, and tenderness for each other.

I brought my need for deep emotional connection into my adult life. And fortunately, in waltzed John Henry Bowen to reveal what love, a relationship, and emotions were like.

John, like Mother, was a people person and fun loving. He had moved into a home down the street from my parents' home while I was in college. He and his roommate, Jim, both worked at the General Motors Technical Center in Warren, Michigan, about a mile from our family home. John and Jim knew our neighbor, Agnes, who had bought her neighbor's home to rent out.

John was allowed to use Agnes' washing machine and clothes dryer each Monday evening after work while Daddy and Agnes' husband were off to a lodge meeting. Mother would visit Agnes most Monday nights, and of course, she met John as he came in and out of the house carrying loads of laundry. Mother, Agnes, and John became fast friends. At home, all we heard was John this and John that! They had fun laughing, joking, and building friendships.

CHAPTER 4: FOUNDATION OF LOVE

During the last half of my junior year of college, I moved home to do my student teaching and then a year-long internship. I worked hard during the day in my classrooms. The teacher preparation program at Michigan State required us to take extension classes to complete our bachelor's in elementary education while we did our student teaching and internship. The classes were immediately after our teaching day. Then in the evening, I had papers to correct and homework to do. Once again, my love of learning, my discipline, and my work ethic came into play. I was committed to completing my degree in four years.

While I was working hard, Mother was getting to know the bachelor down the street. She and Agnes began to plot how they would introduce us. I regularly heard comments like, "It is Halloween night. Why don't you go trick or treating at the bachelors' house." Of course, I never did because I knew they were older and already had careers. I was just twenty-one and they were already thirty-something.

In the fall of 1968, my dad my dad was installed as leader of his lodge. It was a big deal to Daddy. After the ceremony, the organization would celebrate with a meal in the basement of the lodge followed by a small party in our basement for the leadership team and some of Daddy's good friends.

Of course, you can guess who was at this party.

Actually, John was a member of the lodge, but he only attended occasionally. He was an organist and played at some of the lodge meetings. For Daddy's monumental event, John would play the prelude and postlude, and he would accompany the singing during the installation ceremony. His participation in this special event created an opportunity for him to be invited to both parties, the one at the lodge and the after party.

The lodge members' wives had prepared all of the celebration food and organized the assigned seating at the dinner. I was not at all surprised to be seated next to John. (Mother, Agnes, and their friends were at work—matchmakers!) As we ate, I could choose to interact with this handsome bachelor or miss the opportunity of the day by directing my attention to all of the others at the table.

Make no mistake, John made sure I was entertained during dinner and during the party at home.

By the end of the evening, it was apparent we enjoyed each other's company. As John said, "Good-night," he invited me on a date—dinner at a club in Toronto listening to Danny Holly play jazz on the organ. I agreed, and our life-changing romance began!

During his performance, Holly played John's favorite piece, "Satin Doll." That was the theme song of our love life along with "Sadie, Sadie, Married Lady" by Barbra Streisand. Every chance he could, John would put one of those songs on the record player and sing along.

I enjoyed John's fun side, and he was attracted to me and my faith. Since he lived four houses away, I saw him for fleeting moments between tasks most evenings.

Our love quickly blossomed!

After our jaunt to Toronto, John didn't call me until the following Friday evening. He called after work and invited me to go out for pizza. Surprise—I already had a blind date. A classmate's husband was in the Army, and his buddy, Larry, was in town. I had agreed to spend an evening with Larry as a favor to my friend. It was an okay date, but nothing like my first date with John. Larry eventually married another of my college friends, but the date forced John to recognize he better take a stronger lead if he was really interested in me.

That he did. From that day forward, he always made our next date before we parted.

Since I was busy on that Friday night, John offered to attend worship with me on Sunday followed by lunch and a Sunday drive. Faith,

CHAPTER 4: FOUNDATION OF LOVE

fun, hard work, and conversation became the cornerstone of our life together.

John had been married when he was younger. He didn't have children, yet he felt bad about coming into our relationship with divorce on his record and only a GED when I was soon to be a fresh, young college graduate. These topics were foremost in our discussions as we sorted through our hopes, dreams, and feelings. I believed we could make a good life together. After all, he had a lot of training and a good career. My career required a college degree; his did not. We continued dating since I believed we would be good marriage partners.

John was able to help me understand my feelings and emotions as we talked and talked and talked. When I got hurt or angry, he would make me tell him what was wrong. At first, I didn't really know what to say. I was just hurt. Talking about feelings was new to me, but once I started, the dam broke loose and I came to grips with my deep well of emotions. Talking about my feelings was helpful, and having him love me through those painful discussion was crucial in helping me to mature and begin to understand myself.

Since John was thirty-two and I was about to be twenty-two and my education was nearly complete, we decided not to wait to get engaged and married. We met in early November and started dating immediately. We went away on a General Motors' ski club weekend over New Year's and worshiped together every Sunday. Seeing each other every day, we felt ready to move forward and make plans to marry.

One evening in late January of 1969, we walked into my house. Daddy was sitting at the kitchen table working on a crossword puzzle, and Mother was in the family room watching TV. John sat down with my father, and I went into the family room. I could hear some of the conversation at the kitchen table, but Mother was oblivious to what was going on between John and Daddy in the kitchen.

John asked my father for my hand in marriage, and with a few words (true to Daddy), he agreed, but he insisted I had to finish my education. That would be simple since I had about four months left.

Then John stood up, opened the family room door, all smiles, and announced to Mother, "I have just asked Al for Sandy's hand in marriage."

Mother, the talker, turned into the silent one. Mother, the excitable person, sat silent for what seemed like forever. She had been pretty sure an engagement would come, but we had only been dating for two months—although to us it seemed like a lifetime.

Once John's announcement sank in, Mother never stopped talking! It was a fun time, setting a date, meeting with my pastor, planning for my pastor uncle to perform the ceremony, choosing wedding announcements, and on and on. The time flew by for us as we continued to get to know each other and fall deeper in love. It was a love like I had never experienced—a love that filled my parched soul.

Once John asked the question and announced our intentions, John and I began looking at rings in every jewelry store in the local malls, getting an idea of what I would like in a ring. Unbeknownst to me, John had a friend in the jewelry business who could create a custom ring that met my desire. It was made specially for me, and the diamond was chosen for its high quality.

On Valentine's Day 1969, John made reservations for us at a nice Italian restaurant in the Detroit area. He had arranged for us to be in a small, candlelit room with only two small tables. We ate scrumptious food, drank some wine, and held hands—aww, so romantic! He reached into his pocket and pulled out a box with a beautiful marquis diamond ring in it and asked me to marry him. We cried, and I said, "I will!" It was official. I would become Mrs. John Henry Bowen in July.

We finished our desserts and jumped in his car to show my parents the engagement ring—then it was official so Mother could tell the world.

John was a loving, tender man who loved to say, "I love you," hundreds of times a day. Throughout the day, he would call out, "Honey, I love you." We would be at work, across the yard, somewhere in the house, or in the car, and he would call out, "I love you!" I so needed a man like him, a man to tell me over and over and over again what my soul needed to hear. His love was tender, caring, and vocal. I learned what true love felt like, and I discovered what I had been missing all of my life. He adored me and told me I was beautiful. The look in his eye melted my heart, and when he held my hand, I was reminded over and over how much he loved me.

Everyone we knew was so happy for us. John's mom was exuberant about our relationship. Mom loved me and often said, "Thank you for bringing such goodness into my son's life." She loved that I was a teacher and a good mom. She loved her son so much. Growing up while moving from place to place with a harsh military dad had been hard on John. His divorce and transient life in the Navy was not what she wanted for him. She loved John, she loved me, and she adored our children. In fact, she spoiled us with love, repairing our clothes, and making new clothes for us each year when she came to visit. As a sign of our love for Mom, we created a Nana room in each house we would own in Michigan; even though she was only with us a week each year, it was her room.

Being in love is addictive, especially if you have not felt love the way you need to. I needed to feel John's love, hear him say I love you, experience new, fun ways to share life, and spend time just talking. Later, I read *The Five Love Languages* by Gary Chapman and discovered my love language is time spent together and touch. God knew John was the man to meet my deep needs.

Building a Foundation of Love

> *"Above all, love each other deeply,*
> *because love covers over a multitude of sins."*
>
> — 1 Peter 4:8

During our courtship and early years of marriage, we talked a lot about my upbringing and some of the complications within my family. I had struggled with Daddy's emotional distance. John always encouraged me to move past this awkward time in my relationship with Daddy. I had no clue how to do anything other than what I had learned. I had been a small child when the fracture between us happened.

Daddy didn't know how to be playful with little girls, but he wanted daughters so his children wouldn't have to experience the devastation of being drafted to fight in a war. One night when my sister and I were preschoolers, Daddy was playing on the floor tickling us when I began to cry. I distinctly remember him pushing me away and saying, "Get out of here, baby," while he continued to play with my sister. My self-worth was seriously wounded, and I didn't come close to him emotionally until I was well into adulthood. Everything he did with my sister caused that early childhood pain to grow into a mountain I did not know how to climb. In fact, I didn't unearth what happened for fifty years, and then I began to pray about it. I forgave him since he didn't know how he had hurt me.

Ensuring love was at the forefront of our family was important to John and me. We agreed our children would hear us say we loved each other and them. We didn't want them ever to doubt we loved them. We ensured they knew we loved each other by showing our affection through modest hugs and kisses given in front of them. They needed to see as well as hear our love. And we would hold them, hug them, and listen to them. Before our eldest was conceived, we had several conversations about raising a family filled with love in all ways.

John always made a point of teaching our children to treasure me. He would say, "Doesn't she look beautiful today?" or "I love Mommy's new haircut, dress, or shoes." He would walk into the house at dinnertime and make a positive comment about the smell of dinner, the clean house, or the nicely set dinner table. Words of affirmation were part of our life because we ensured they were. And we wanted our children to be part of those affirmations.

He took great joy in planning breakfast in bed for me every Mother's Day and preparing a meal for the moms in my family, including my mother, my sister, and me. He would buy presents for them and me and bring our children into some of those plans. He would barbeque and plan out and prepare the rest of the meal. Mother's Day was for all mothers to be blessed and not have to work in the kitchen. This tradition continued even after John was no longer physically present. My children made me breakfast in bed, planned a gift, made a card, and decided what we would do for lunch. In fact, one year they saved all of their money from doing chores to hire a limousine for the four of us to have a special day. They treated me to a fancy restaurant, bought a nice necklace for me, and took me on a ride to local vineyards. We ended up at an upscale ice cream parlor for dessert before returning home. John would have been so proud of them.

Love was the center of our household in so many ways, along with honor and teamwork. Love is not always easy. It is hard work when things are overwhelming, but love will get you through. John's love helped me explore God's love, and it carried the kids and me through in the days, months, and years after his death.

I am so grateful now that we had the wherewithal to make an intentional plan to reveal love to our children in a wholesome family way. Our household was full of love, for us as a couple and for each of our children. Love expanded to friends and family, neighbors, and even the puppies we would have years later. No matter your age, consider making a plan to show love and make it a foundational piece of your life.

Reflection Time

How was love a part of your childhood foundation?
_____
_____
_____

How have you carried love forward as an adult?
_____
_____
_____

Are you intentional about expressing love verbally and physically (hugging) and learning what pleases others?
_____
_____
_____

Do you feel loved? Who loves you?
_____
_____
_____

Prayer Time

Pray about your young life, asking God to help you remember times when you were deeply loved and times when you felt rejected. Then embrace the good memory and ask God to heal your heart and soul where you felt rejected. Pray you can feel more love and give out more love now.

Closing Words About Exploring Your Foundation

I have been writing about the foundations of our family. Faith, the character of blending families, hard work, teamwork, and love were our family's strengths when John was alive. These ways were our foundation when we were forced to move forward in new ways as a family of four.

Dearly Beloved, as you live your life, consider the generations to follow. Are you modeling a good life for them? Are you living a disciplined life that is obvious to those who love you? Are faith, the character traits of blending lives, hard work, teamwork, love, and education part of your foundation? If not, what are your foundational pieces?

Pray, asking God to reveal what your Foundational strengths are on which your life stands.

_____
_____
_____
_____
_____
_____

With those core intentional plans, you can do pretty much anything. You and your family can ride the waves of highs and lows, joys and devastation. With a foundation as hard as a rock to stand on, you and yours will be kept from sinking.

Season 2

Building the Framework Securely on the Foundation

"By the grace God has given me, I laid a foundation as a wise builder, and someone else is building on it. But each one should build with care."

— 1 Corinthian 3:10

A Foundation was laid down for me. I was responsible for building on that solid Foundation of Faith, Education, Teamwork, Hard Work, Blended Roots, and Love. Each of these Foundational pieces was in place for the Framework of my adult life to build upon. The Framework has four walls: Family and Personal Friends, Church Family, Finances, and Prayer. The Family/Friends were the west wall and our Church Family was the east wall of my home. Finances were the south wall, and Prayer the north, where the door is always open for Jesus to come in. The Cornerstone on the northeast corner is Surrender.

The Foundational pieces were each important for the building of the walls upon them. It took Faith, Education, Character, and Love to build this upright structure. Some of the walls were built as a couple, and some when I was single. Each was built further along my journey, and I thank God for every part of this structure that allows me to balance tragedy, loss, single parenting, my career, our home, and my inner healing. Without any of these components, life would have been much more fragile. God's grace helped me every step of the way.

Setting the Scene—Walking Through Loss

"In this way they will lay up treasure for themselves as a firm foundation for the coming age, so that they may take hold of the life that is truly life."

— 1 Timothy 6:19

Our family began to unravel one spring day in 1985. I was teaching science to my fourth-grade students one afternoon when the principal walked in and told me there was a phone call for me in the office. She would watch my class so I could take the call. It was strange because people never called me at school. While walking to the office, my thoughts went in every direction. My children were in two different schools, and not in the school where I taught. My mother-in-law lived locally, but she wouldn't call me at school. The principal would have just taken a message if it were not serious. She had given me no clue about the nature of the call.

It was John's mom. She told me John had passed out at work and been taken to Kaiser Hospital in Sacramento. She said she would pick up the girls, who were eight and ten at the time, after school and take them home. My son, who was twelve, would ride his bike home as usual, and Mom would stay with the three of them until I got home.

What happened next is a blank other than the challenge of finding Kaiser Hospital. I had never been to this hospital before and had no clue how to find it. This was pre-GPS and pre-cellphone. Mom told me the name of the street, and I located the hospital on the map. It felt like I was driving across country. In my panic, I could not get there quick enough.

When I finally arrived, I parked the car at the emergency department entrance and ran in to find John. First, I found John's work friend, who had followed him to the hospital. The friend said John had gone to the men's room at work because he didn't feel well. He was in a stall, had a seizure, and passed out on the floor. Someone walked into the men's room and found John there. John was taken to the hospital in an ambulance. That was all John's friend knew at the time. We sat staring at the floor in the emergency room waiting for someone to call me in to see John and speak with the doctor.

When I did see John, it was devastating to see him feeling so horrible. The doctor said they had run some tests and taken x-rays and a CAT scan. They knew he'd had a seizure, but they didn't know why. They sent us home with some medication and instructions to make an appointment with his primary care doctor to follow up.

I helped John dress, and they wheeled him out while I retrieved our station wagon. We thanked our friend and sent him on his way. Then we made the hour-long drive back to our home in Vacaville. In the car, we talked about the day, and it was all puzzling to John. He'd had a good morning at work, had lunch with a friend, gone back to the office and begun to work. Soon, he had a terrible headache and felt strange. The next thing he knew, he was in the hospital. All the way home, he sat wondering about the minutes and hours between his last memory and waking up in the hospital.

When we arrived home, our children and his mom were excited to see him. John and I had a bite to eat, Mom went home, and soon it was time for the children to go to bed. With them tucked in and their nighttime prayers prayed, John and I sat in the family room talking. I sat in the recliner, and he sat on the floor, as he often did.

Suddenly, in the middle of a sentence, John's eyes rolled back, and he passed out again. Oh no!

The doctor had said, "If there are any more symptoms, call us." So, I did. They told me to bring him back to Sacramento! Mom came back over to be with the children, and we headed back to the hospital. I would travel there many times over the next couple of years.

Once at the hospital again, the doctors ran more tests and decided to admit John. Driving away from the hospital that night, I had no idea what a roller-coaster ride I would be on in the days and weeks ahead.

More tests, more x-rays, scans, and medication, but the doctors still didn't know what was happening. Could it be epilepsy? They didn't know. No mention of a brain tumor was made, and it never crossed our minds. Finally, John was released with anti-seizure medication and cautioned not to drive. That put us in a pickle because he worked an hour from home. John decided to trust the medication and continue to go to work. But the medication changed him a lot. He was sleepier and grouchier. Often John would leave the office early or make his business trips in the direction of Vacaville so he could come home early to nap before dinner.

John lacked energy for life, and his endurance decreased. I took him to doctor appointments. His neurologist attributed his symptoms to "side effects of the medication" and said, "Let's try another medication." John didn't have any more seizures, but our lives began to take a drastic turn for the worse. Our once active, fun-loving family slowed down. John was much less active in our lives and less emotionally present.

Then in the spring of 1985, Mom was discovered to have liver cancer. She was gone in just a few months. Actually, she died July 27, 1985, one day after our sixteenth wedding anniversary.

Her death left me the sole caregiver of John and my children. I felt like the weight of the world was resting on my shoulders because Mom had been such an important part of our California lives. We all missed her so much. This loss would turn me toward my church family and the Lord more every day.

Fortunately, I had the foundations of faith, character of blending lives, hard work, teamwork, education, and love I described in earlier chapters to lean on. Those foundations were seriously tested. Even though I had faith in the Lord as my Savior, and we had a place of worship, I didn't know much more about the Lord and His constant presence in my life. The foundation of hard work took over, and fortunately, I had the foundation of education to stand solidly on. My teaching career was solid; it brought in consistent income and provided us with medical benefits. As a teaching professional, I was able to leave my worries at the door to be present for my students. In fact, one of my student's parents wrote a letter to be put in my file at the district office saying how she knew I was going through a lot in my personal life, but her son's education was not negatively affected at all. In fact, I was a blessing to him.

My teaching career was helpful during this crisis season of our family's life because I could leave work at 3:15 or 3:30 p.m., taking work home with me. This allowed me to be present with my family and handle schoolwork once our family was settled for the evening. My boss was kind and flexible with my situation, and the staff was an incredible blessing.

During the spring of 1986, John's health had settled into a new normal—he was slower and sleepy, but the seizures had not recurred. The doctor ordered a new medication for him to try, but John decided to wait to take it because the school year was almost over and the children and I were going to travel across the country to visit family in Michigan. John had been laid off from his Sacramento job, and he had begun a business with his friend, Karen, supplying small local markets and gas stations with bags, cash register tape, and other paper products. Therefore, he decided to stay home to work on his business. The rest of us were on summer vacation and planned to be gone for four weeks. One week driving across country, two weeks in Michigan visiting friends and family, and one week to return home.

We loaded our cartop carrier with camping gear and the back of our station wagon with four painted beer cases that held most of our clothing. The plan was to visit Salt Lake City, stay near Yellowstone, and visit Mount Rushmore and many other attractions along the way. During this trip, we would combine camping and motel stops, creating the trip of a lifetime. John and I had seen many of the places we visited on our honeymoon seventeen years earlier.

Off we went, waving goodbye to John and our dog, Ebony. I felt secure knowing John had done well since the two incidents the previous year.

We hadn't been back to visit since we left Michigan in June 1983. It was time to reconnect with our loved ones, including my parents, who traveled from Florida to be with us in Michigan, and the rest of our Michigan church friends.

The trip was amazing! We saw so many wonderful sites along the route. Our AAA maps were a great asset, and the children became very familiar with the TripTiks directing our route. After six days of travel, we pulled into the driveway of my sister's apartment. Mother and Daddy were there to greet us, along with my nephew. My sister would soon be home from work.

Mother and Daddy slept in my nephew's room, my sister in her bedroom, and the children slept on couches or air mattresses. I stayed nearby with a good friend, Eleanor; her husband was deceased, and her children were grown. She had two spare rooms; one became mine, and one was available for my children if they needed to have a break from the crowded apartment.

The two weeks flew by with family time, visiting friends, and meals with friends and family. On the Friday before we were to drive home, we spent the day with my college friends Jane and Larry at their cottage. Their daughters were there along with my friends Kathy and Phil and their two children. Larry treated the children and Phil to a boat ride, inner tubing, and playing in the water while we girls had a gab fest and organized dinner. After dinner, we all sat around telling embarrassing college stories to each other's children. It was fun, but before we knew it, we had to head back.

The children and I would stay at my friend Eleanor's home that night because it was late when we returned to the area from the lake house where we had spent the day. We all fell asleep quickly.

At about 2:00 a.m., Eleanor knocked on the bedroom door and said, "Someone is on the phone for you."

Oh, no! It was another ominous phone call, causing a knot in my stomach. It was our neighbor, Pat. She said John had been taken to Kaiser Hospital in Vallejo. Another neighbor saw the ambulance and knew John was home alone. She ran to Pat's house to tell her. Pat was a very close friend and a nurse.

Pat ran across the street before they loaded John into the ambulance to see what was happening. She took his wallet to give information to the hospital and said she would be there soon. In the house, she noticed the two rolodexes on our kitchen counter were open. Our personal one was open to Eleanor's home, and the business one was opened to John's partner, Karen. Pat called Karen and asked her to meet her at the hospital. Then she called me at Eleanor's to tell me what was happening. She would take the number with her and keep me informed.

I couldn't go back to sleep. Eleanor and I sat up talking until the children awoke. I told them what happened and then called my parents.

Then we waited.

Pat checked in, but she had little information. She finally got a doctor to call me. In the meantime, Pat and Karen became my sisters so they could get family information about what was happening to John. We were all blonds, so I guess we could have passed as sisters if we were together.

Pat was concerned because they had John on a gurney in the hallway and didn't seem to be doing anything for him as he lay there in pain. Being a nurse, she kept asking questions gaining little information. Then in the middle of the night, they transported John to Kaiser Sacramento so he could be treated by a neurologist.

Mother and Daddy thought it was best for us to fly home, and Brent, John's best friend, offered to drive our station wagon back to us when he could get off of work.

It was quite a sight when we showed up at the airport with four beer cases painted green and plastered with contact paper flowers. My hanging clothes were put in a cardboard box for me before we boarded the plane. Since we bought the tickets at the last minute, we were not sitting together, although my youngest was in the row right in front of me. That was so helpful since she was only eight.

The trip home seemed like eternity, but fortunately we were greeted in Sacramento by Pat, Karen, and their husbands. We would go to the hospital to see John, then have some dinner before heading home. I was glad to have them with us as we arrived at the hospital once again.

I made the long trip down the hallway alone to greet John. Seeing John was a very challenging experience. We had left home three weeks earlier, leaving behind our handsome, caring daddy/husband and returned to find a bald, nearly blind, bloated man who did not look like John at all. They had shaved his head and given him steroids to help with the swelling and head pain. The doctors had him on a no liquid, no food regimen to bring down the swelling so they could do more tests. He was hooked up to so many monitors that his room looked like the cockpit of an airplane. It was rather intimidating!

John was so thirsty from this regimen that they called the Sahara Desert treatment. All he could do was suck on small, wet sponges for moisture. This treatment was to help eliminate the excess fluid on his brain. Despite the situation, we were so happy to see each other. We exchanged lots of love and tears as I learned what to expect in the days ahead.

I brought the children in to greet Daddy. It was such a confusing time for them—the oldest had just turned thirteen. They were happy to see Daddy, but the machines and John's appearance were overwhelming to them.

Everyone else had quick visits, and then we were off to get dinner and go home.

The days and weeks ahead were filled with tests and treatment of the large brain tumor found in John's head. It was the shape of a hand and between the skull and the brain. The surgery would remove the lion's share of the tumor, and radiation treatments would begin once he had recovered more from the surgery.

As the new school year approached, we were focused on the massive decisions we had to make regarding John's health. The surgery was considered a success, but it did not remove all of the tumor. Next, John had to endure six weeks of radiation treatments in an attempt to destroy the remainder of the tumor. Life's roller coaster continued.

A Downward Turn

The year flew by with us continually grasping at hope—hope that John's body was healing like the doctors said it was, hope our prayers would be granted, hope and peace in our own prayers, hope because that was all we had, hope that Daddy would still be there as our children grew up. But our hope was dashed when John's symptoms began to return in March.

I took John to the doctor for several check-ups. The doctor said, "It takes time for the brain to heal. Be patient." But the doctor was not with us daily as we watched John's ability to walk decline. He slept more and was frustrated with life. I took John for chiropractic treatments regularly to help ease his back pain, and the chiropractor commented on John dragging his left leg.

After much asking around, I found an oncology brain specialist at the University of San Francisco Medical Center. This hospital is a teaching and experimental hospital. The doctor asked for John's medical records. He also requested another MRI. It took several weeks for me to gather everything, but at long last, we had an appointment scheduled for May 26, 1987. I borrowed a neighbor's van and a wheelchair. I took the children out of school. My mother was in town helping us as we finished the school year. The six of us piled into the van with the wheelchair and headed to San Francisco. The plan was to have a picnic at a park along San Francisco Bay, meet the doctor, and then have dinner in San Francisco. It was my fortieth birthday, and John wanted us to have seafood to celebrate.

After the doctor examined all the records, x-rays, and MRIs, he called us into his office. The images were displayed on his well-lit wall boards. He showed us that the tumor had returned in the middle of John's brain in the March x-rays. Then he showed us the progress over the next two months. The neuro-oncology specialist informed us that John had only a short time to live. After he explained the entire situation, he offered us an experimental chemotherapy that we agreed to try. The experimental medication would be given to our Kaiser oncologist, who was an acquaintance of this doctor. The arrangement was the UC San Francisco doctor would provide the experimental drugs, and the oncologist at Kaiser would oversee the treatment and provide a secondary drug. John would take pills for two weeks; then the Kaiser doctor would come to our home to administer the experimental chemotherapy. After a week free of treatments, the regime would start again.

We agreed to this treatment on the condition that John's quality of life would be the same or better. If he felt horrible, we would stop and enjoy the time we still had together. John's system handled the treatment well, and life moved forward. John was in a hospital bed in our family room by then, and the family room moved to the living room.

He needed his quiet space, and we all needed a place to relax and/or watch TV.

The next three weeks flew by with end-of-year activities and programs, report cards, and cumulative record files to be completed. On Friday, June 13, school was finally over, and we had time to rest. That we did. We decided to celebrate Father's Day that weekend because we had often celebrated Father's Day and my mother's birthday on the same day many times when we had all lived in Michigan. It would be fun for us to have the combined celebration again. John was very hungry for oysters on the half shell, but there were none to be found in Vacaville. Pat worked in Vallejo, on the far end of the Bay. On Monday, she found a seafood restaurant and brought him an oyster dinner to celebrate a belated Father's Day. He ate half of the meal, saving the rest for the next day. Oh, he was so happy! He ate like a little piggy that day!

The yard had grown out of control during the final weeks of school, so I began the process of trimming bushes, cutting grass, and weeding. On Wednesday, June 17, the nurse's aide arrived in the morning to give John a bath, haircut, and shave. The nurse checked on John, who was fine other than having trouble breathing because of fluid on his lungs. She taught him how to breathe with shallow breaths and relax.

After lunch, the girls were with friends at the community center pool, our son was playing basketball with friends in the neighborhood, I was working in the backyard, and Mother was busy in the house.

"Come!" she suddenly called to me through the screen door.

I ran inside.

"He's gone."

I laid my head on John's chest. He was not breathing.

My heart dropped to the ground, and everything went blank as I lingered next to him.

Then I heard the doorbell ring. It was the oncologist from Kaiser coming to give John the chemo shot. God's timing was absolutely perfect. The doctor came in and checked John, pronouncing him dead. The doctor called the mortuary where I had made prior arrangements and stayed with me until John was taken away.

In the meantime, the mortician called the church office since the mortician was a church member also. And the chain of contacts began—the chain of provision and love.

After the doctor and hearse left, I went out to get the mail. Just then, a teacher friend pulled up in front of the house. She had baked cookies for us. As I walked toward her car, she asked, "What's wrong?" I told her John has passed away. "What can I do for you?" I asked, "Could you go pick up my daughters for me at the community center pool?" My daughters knew her well; her classroom was next door to mine, and they had been in my classroom after school every night until it was time to go home. My girls would go with her. Her help was a tremendous gift from God. God's favor was growing increasingly apparent in this terrible time of devastation.

As my teacher friend drove away, a stream of people from church began to arrive. First was our youth pastor, Pastor Phil, who would walk with me to find my son and inform him of the loss of his father. Thank God Pastor Phil was with us because it was devasting for my son to hear this news standing near his street basketball friends.

During John's illness, we had also had the support of Stephen Ministers. Stephen Ministries is a Christian educational organization that trains church members to accompany those facing a life crisis. It was founded in 1975 in St. Louis, Missouri, by the psychologist Reverend Kenneth C. Haugk. Now, among the people who joined us in the hours after John's death were my Stephen Minister, Carol, and my daughter's Stephen Minister, Krissy. We were also visited by the youth ministry secretary, Pat H., and other leaders from Bible Study. Soon, a dozen people were with us. All of us were devastated since John was so loved by many people.

When my daughter arrived, she was met by loving people. Krissy was able to spend time with my daughter, and Pastor Phil spent time with my son. My youngest snuggled next to her grandmother as I handled the rest, telling the story of the afternoon. Food began to arrive, and others went out to buy meals from KFC. The stream of love, provision, and care was so steady that even though this was the worst day of our lives, God's presence and provision were everywhere.

Later, our friends went home, leaving us alone to regroup. Then we heard, "Yahoo!" That was Pat's call at the door as she returned from work. She came to see John before she went home to make dinner. Of course, we had a cry with Pat, who was so close to our family—God had blessed us with a caring, loving nurse as a part of our family. She was so helpful during John's illness, on this day of loss, and in the days to follow.

Soon we headed to bed to try to rest. I really wanted space to be alone. My head was spinning with the loss and all the arrangements I had to make, people to call, flowers to be ordered, a funeral service to plan, and on and on and on.

At long last, I slept only to wake groggy and exhausted, but there was little time to waste. My sister, nephew, and father made arrangements to fly in on Friday. The viewing was to start at 4:00 p.m. on Friday; the funeral would be on Saturday at 11:00 a.m.

A fellow teacher whose husband had passed away when her children were young talked to me about how her children were able to handle the saying goodbye process. Each family member chose an object to place in the casket to represent some part of their relationship with their father as a final goodbye present. I spoke with our children, and we agreed we would do the same. It was helpful for us to look at the fun parts of our lives with John and choose objects like a golf ball, a softball, a crocheted Jelly Belly duck, and a soft foam-shaped heart he had held many times during his bedrest. A couple of us wrote letters to John.

Our family arrived early to the funeral home to have time alone with John's body. Each of us placed our gifts in his coffin and talked about what they meant, and those who wrote letters read them aloud and placed them into his hands.

Then, we all held hands, and I prayed.

We were so grateful to have these positive things to focus on during this devastatingly difficult evening.

Finally, Saturday arrived, and we made our way to the church. We greeted people, said goodbye to John one last time before the casket was closed, and then met in the library as a family with Pastor Phil. Pastor Phil said the prayer.

The emptiness was overwhelming, yet I was at peace because John was with the Lord. John wanted us to celebrate, and he wanted to wear his yellow Hawaiian shirt. We honored that request. Pastor Phil led the service as a celebration of the life of John Henry Bowen and the presence of the Lord in his life.

The sanctuary was packed with friends, family, coworkers, business friends, neighbors, fellow teachers, and the church choir. John's life was celebrated, God was honored, and we got through the day as we were able. More provision was given to us by our congregation during our fellowship time with friends, and at home, our former congregation brought a spaghetti meal for the family who would be at home with us. Everywhere we turned, God showed up with love and provision.

The Framework of church families and the love of all we knew in so many places surrounded our family that day. They had lost a beloved friend too.

I have to mention one other sign of God's plan in the final week of John's life. The staff at my school agreed to bring us food for the month of June. The calendar was filled in with a different staff member's name for every day of the month—except two. My boss was sorry about the two blank days, but I told her it was fine. Surely, we would have plenty of leftovers or could fend for ourselves for two days.

Those days were June 17 and June 20, the day John died and the day of the funeral. Of course, when the days were left blank, no one knew the time or date of John's death. As it turned out, the day of his passing, neighbors and others brought plenty of food. Likewise, on the day of his funeral, no food was needed. The church took care of food that day. God's plans are perfect in all ways.

Chapter 5
Framework of Family/Friends

"Give proper recognition to those widows who are really in need. But if a widow has children or grandchildren, these should learn first of all to put their religion into practice by caring for their own family and so repaying their parents and grandparents, for this is pleasing to God. The widow who is really in need and left all alone puts her hope in God and continues night and day to pray and ask God for help."

— 1 Timothy 5:3-5

John was a people person. He made friends easily wherever we were. This was a tremendous asset in building our east wall. Our friends were like family, and united with his mom, my parents, and our children, provided a solid wall around us. Friends and family intertwined with our life and built a welcoming wall around us all of our married life, which continued when I was single after John's passing.

In the early years of our marriage, my parents, sister, and extended family were an active part of our life. John's mom was a tremendous support and an encourager, but she lived in California, and we lived in Michigan. In 1983, we packed up our household and made the cross-country trek to live near John's mom in the northern Californian town of Vacaville. It was wonderful to live near Mom. She was full of joy, love, and appreciation for me in her son's life. Mom was a treasure in helping us with our children when the need arose. She was there when John had his first seizure, stepping in to pick up the children from school and coming over when I had to drive to the hospital in Sacramento.

Unfortunately, as we were dealing with John's progressive illness, Mom discovered she had liver cancer and died within four months of the discovery. It was tragic for our family because we loved her so. John was the executor of her estate and planned her funeral. Having gone through this with John and listening to his thoughts made it much easier when I had to plan his farewell two years later. I spoke with the same people at the funeral home and the cemetery. When life was at its toughest, I had his plans, his works, and his thoughts to rely upon.

Mom was always an important part of our family wall. We created a bedroom in both of our homes for Nana, even though she would only use it once a year. It was Nana's room. Our children adored Nana, and we continue to talk about her preciousness to all of us.

My parents were an integral part of our married life since they lived within five minutes of John's work. We lived a half hour from them and would often stop by to share life. Their house was always our holiday home until they moved to Florida in 1980. Our house was the Mother's Day and birthday house. John and I loved to have the family together, and my parents so enjoyed their grandchildren. We were puzzled when they chose to move to Florida, but they enjoyed some of the best years of their lives as a couple there.

Once they moved to Florida, I am sad to say, the distance in miles created an emotional distance as well. Yet when we faced the crisis of John's illness, they stepped up to the plate. Daddy helped us get home when John had his grand mal seizure. Daddy bought our plane tickets and took us to the airport. From afar, we kept in touch, updating them about John's health. Mother so loved John and was distraught over this tragedy. When the time came that I needed help, she got on a plane and came to be his constant helper. Bless her heart. How many mothers-in-law will change their son-in-law's diaper? She was with him for hours during the last weeks of school. And she was there the day he drew his last breath. It broke her heart terribly to roll him over after changing his diaper and see he was no longer breathing.

I am so grateful for my parents and all they put into raising me, loving my family, and caring for us in the last year of John's life.

Then there were the friends, too many to mention all. One that stands out is Brent, John's best friend from General Motors. We loved him and his wife, Bett, and they so loved our family. Brent was the one who drove our station wagon across the country to bring it to us when the kids and I flew back to be with John. It was an amazing, generous gift! Brent and Bett taught me so much about friendship and love.

John and I spent countless hours full of love and laughter with Brent and his wife Bett. They treasured our children, showing up for their baptisms, and later, they spoiled us with a day of laughter and joy when we traveled to Michigan. I am forever grateful for them.

Secure in the love of family and friends, I stepped into the final year of John's life and then my widowhood with confidence in the support God had provided. Thank God for love, family, and friends!

Church Family

"My command is this: Love each other as I have loved you. Greater love has no one than this: to lay down one's life for one's friends."

— John 15:12-13

Fortunately, we also had the foundation of our congregation, who cared for us since my family lived across the country, John's mom was gone, and his brother lived in Arizona. Our church family carried us along as the four of us held things together while John recovered and then after he passed. Without our church family, we would have been truly lost.

Many people we did not know brought meals to us. Others took John to radiation treatments and Bible studies. When he was feeling better, two gentlemen drove John to another town to socialize with others who had serious brain issues. Three of us had Stephen Ministers who listened to us and prayed with us. Others came to repaint the hallway to cover John's fingerprints from his many trips up the steps grasping onto the wall. Others drove the children to events, called, and cared for us.

Looking back, we saw God's provisions for our family when we didn't know we would need such help. In January of 1986, God led John and I to a new church on the other side of town. We looked for a large church with a youth group for our son who was entering seventh grade. That decision was truly one of God's provisions and our saving grace through that difficult year. Our children were in the kids and youth programs, and I was getting to know some of the adults when the crisis happened. The women's group, youth ministry, the pastors, the daytime Bible study group, and many others banded around us however they could.

Our other church offered much support also. It was a small church, and we hadn't left with ill will. We had many friends there, yet it was just not a large enough church to provide the support we would need over the weeks and years ahead. The Framework of church bodies along with many of the camp leaders became our strength. The west wall included so many church families who grieved with us in the end. They had lost a beloved friend too.

The church was so generous to us. When John died, the choir robed up and sang a special song. Pastor Phil was a solid, loving support to us during this week and after. The ladies of the church provided finger sandwiches and cookies for all who had gathered for the celebration of John's life. We felt cared for by the loving arms of the Lord's people, our friends, and loved ones.

Reflection Time

Do you have solid structures around you in family, friends, and church family? Describe your support system. Who are they, and how do you support each other?

_____
_____
_____

How do you nurture those important relationships? Are they a strength for you?

_____
_____
_____

Write how you might strengthen the relationships you have in your life.

_____
_____
_____

In times of great need, people often step forward to help those in crisis. That is so important. It is important for us to understand the ways we can reach out to those around us with love and relationship.

Prayer Time

Talk to God about your life and relationships. Ask Him what you might do to strengthen them or reach out to those who appear to be alone. You might want to ask God to open your heart wider to reach others who need a smile, a hug, or to know someone cares. What you give always comes back in greater ways.

Chapter 6

Framework of Financial Preparation

"And my God will meet all your needs according to the riches of His glory in Christ Jesus."
— Philippians 4:19

Raising a family on my own was daunting, especially the financial piece. During the first week after John's death, as I sat in my overwhelming grief and pain, a nagging thought crept forward, *How will the four of us live in California on my teacher's pay? Soon there will be high school expenses and post high school education. How, Lord?*

In those days, I did not have the full understanding of God as the provider for widows and orphans. I had carried a lot of the financial burden over the years as John's jobs came and went, especially during the final two-and-a-half years of his life. Fortunately, I had job security as a teacher. I was well educated and respected in the teaching field. When John died, I had been with the Vacaville Unified School District for four years, which gave me district tenure and steady, year-round income and benefits. Looking back, I am grateful for the family foundation of education and Daddy's financial preparation to support our post high school studies. I was grateful for the ten years of teaching in Michigan and the references I brought with me that quickly opened doors. I am grateful that John and I saved our pennies so I might earn my master's degree in elementary education. With that degree, I was allowed to teach in California as soon as I passed the certification test, which I took and passed before we arrived in California.

The foundation of education prior to marriage and our investment in future education was the key to financial security. I knew I could put a roof over my family's head and food on the table, yet it would be basic as a teacher. We had sacrificed my Michigan teacher's higher income to move to a new, exciting state near John's family. I figured the tradeoff would be worth it as I worked up the pay scale in Vacaville Unified School District and became tenured in California. At that point in my California teaching career, I had solid income, but nothing extra for frills.

Another wall of our financial framework was put in place early in our marriage—we invested in a whole life insurance policy for John through Aid Association for Lutherans before we had children. The agents in the insurance company were family friends. When I called Fred, our agent, after John's death, he expressed his grief for our loss and assured us he would help us in any way we needed help. The first way was to contact the home office in Wisconsin to file the claim on John's policy. Soon after that call, Fred delivered a check personally, along with his tender care and a hug. I felt so cared for, and I was grateful we had placed this part of our financial Framework around our family eighteen years prior, especially with a caring Christian insurance company. This check would help us move forward, but it was not enough for many more years of education and life with children at home.

The week after John died, I received his June disability check in the mail. With every check there was a warning statement enclosed, "In the event of the death of the recipient, the Social Security Office must be contacted, and the check returned. Do not deposit or cash the check as it is owned by the recipient on the check." My heart sank because that monthly income was so helpful in sustaining our family while John had no income. His business was struggling in his absence, and Karen had every right to keep whatever income there was since she was the one working the business. When John's disability payments had finally been approved, we were given some peace. When the June check arrived, I sat there staring at it with a huge lump in my stomach. It had to be returned, and there would be no more.

I contacted the local Social Security office to inform them of John's death, and the precious woman who answered the call said, "Go ahead and deposit the check, and the remainder of the June check will be mailed to you within the month." My response was, "Ma'am, you don't understand. John has died. We can no longer receive this check." She explained that we, as a family, would receive monthly death benefits for each of us. I would receive spousal benefits as the sole caregiver of our children, and they would each receive payments until they were eighteen. You can imagine how overwhelmed with joy I was. Even in John's death, there was provision, first from the life insurance and now from death benefits. "Lord, thank you. We will be okay for now." The framework placed around us throughout our marriage and the paperwork we completed to get his disability insurance provided income equal to and, in fact, greater than John had ever earned.

Beloved, never neglect preparation in all ways including, and very importantly, financially. We were not rolling in dough, but we had enough income to keep our quality of life from decaying. With what we received due to John's death, we were able to buy our own house again. Security now surrounded us both financially and with a residence of our very own. Ah! Hallelujah, Peace! Peace in the Financial Framework, the Family Framework, my Career Framework, and our Church Family Framework, the way John and I had lived in preparation for the future we didn't know would unfold as it did was a godsend to me in lifting the burden of concern that was all around me upon John's death.

Our life had had many financial ups and downs over the years, but my consistent career sustained us through every storm, and we had made some very good decisions to nail down a safer framework than I even realized.

Reflection Time

Are your foundational pieces in place to help or enhance your wall building for a new season of your life?

_____
_____
_____

My educational foundation, including my master's degree, was a great asset for us as we moved to California to start a new, fresh life near John's mom. What assets have you placed in your life that give you security? What might you need to do to strengthen those assets to ensure your walls are secure and strong?

_____
_____
_____

Prayer Time

Ask God what you might need to know about your financial walls. What might you need to do to build them more securely? Pray for peace, joy, and strength in all areas of the Framework phase of your life.

Chapter 7
Framework of Prayer

"Call to me and I will answer you and tell you great and unsearchable things you do not know."
— Jeremiah 33:3

"Devote yourselves to prayer, being watchful and thankful."
— Colossians 4:2

Now comes the north wall of the Framework—prayer—where the front door is located. The door is located on this wall for Jesus to enter. I had grown up with prayer. First, we learned a special family prayer that we said before we ate: "Abba, liebe, Vater, Amen."

- Abba means, Daddy or Papa, which was the word Jesus used to speak to God at times.
- Liebe is German for love.
- Daddy love, then Vater which is German for Father.
- Amen which means "so be it."

"Daddy, love, Father, so be it!" Was our first prayer, which was spoken before all meals when I was a child. This form of prayer brought intimacy with the Lord, but none of us really understood that. We called unto Papa with love saying, "So be it."

My sister and I learned this prayer as soon as we were able to talk. Mother taught a hundred children in her day care program to say that prayer. We taught my children, and they taught their children. Daddy, love, Father, so be it. What a blessed way to learn to pray. That prayer was followed by, "Now I lay me down to sleep, I pray the Lord my soul to keep." Every night before bed, our family said that prayer.

My entire family—parents, grandparents, aunts, uncles, and cousins—all said another prayer before meals once the little ones said, "Abba, liebe, Vater, Amen." Everyone in the family recited, "Come, Lord Jesus, be our guest, to these thy gifts to us be blessed. Amen." And at the end of dinner, we recited, "Oh, give thanks unto the Lord, for He is good, and His mercies endure forever."

Soon after that, we learned the Lord's Prayer.

Rote prayer was the staple of our family life, everywhere in my father's family and ours. In fact, if I were to have a meal with my cousins, I imagine we would say the "Come, Lord Jesus" prayer. It was a strong part of our lives and ways, yet we didn't think much about what we were saying. Even so, these prayers were important to us and our family. I believe God appreciated our family tradition, but I also believe He wanted more from us.

For example, our prayers needed to evolve with words from our hearts and to be used in more situations than bedtime and meals. When my son was about three years old, my grandmother was dying of abdominal cancer. My parents, John, my two oldest children, and I visited my grandmother, who was staying in my Aunt Lou's home. I spent some time with Grandma alone, holding her hand and talking. When each of her grandchildren came to visit her, she gave us a gift. Often it was something we had given her. Grandma and I loved to embroider linens. She gave me all of her pillowcases that needed to be finished, the basket I had given her to hold all of her embroidery thread, and some crocheted lace to sew onto some of these pillowcases. I was to pass them along to Grandma's younger grandchildren when they got married. This was a special time between us as we talked and shared our love, but frankly, I never thought to pray with her, even though we often shared our faith. Prayer such as this was not a part of my upbringing.

Soon we were all gathered in the living room, my aunt and uncle, their two children, my parents, John, our children, and me. It was Christmastime, and we talked about the beauty of the tree and joked with each other a bit. In the midst of a lull in the conversation, we noticed my son was in the room with Grandma, holding her hand. Remember, he was three years old. He called her "Schatzee," which is "sweetheart" in German. He said, "Schatzee, would you like to pray?" and we all stopped as we listened to this little one and Schatzee praying the Lord's Prayer. We all sat there with tears in our eyes. What a tender moment, one that taught me the importance of prayer at one's bedside.

What my grandma needed was someone to pray with her, and our three-year-old was the one to do so. For me that was a conviction. I had been bold in making sure prayer was part of our family's upbringing as it had been when I was growing up. I had also prayed silently as a child in some situations. I would talk to God about things, but I had never thought to pray with someone ill or anyone out of our normal context of prayer. We prayed rote prayers before meals, before bed, and at church; otherwise, prayer was not on our minds.

Yet, I must say, I am so grateful that rote prayer was a part of our Foundation. It was a steppingstone for more and more in the future, not only for me, but for my children as they grew into adulthood and for their children who are all teenagers.

At one point in our marriage, John and I took a class at church about living life as a Christian. We must have been challenged to pray together as a couple. I remember asking John if we could pray together before we fell asleep. His answer was, "Okay, but you do the praying."

We did that on occasion, but my bubble was burst a bit in his refusal to pray aloud with me. That is where we were when he became ill. I knew rote prayers, listened to hundreds of prayers at church, and used my prayer book at times to read prayers for specific situations.

Our family crisis pushed me to praying more and more every day. Prayer was growing in my mind, heart, and desire. Yet I must admit that prayer was a component of my life, not at the center of my ways. We comfortably tucked prayer in at mealtime and bedtime, but never had a thought about it at any other time. I had worship in my life on Sundays, prayer as I had been taught, Christian character as a way of life (sort of, at least the legalistic way I learned from my family), yet I made my own life decisions, and far too often it was the way the world decides, thinks, and lives. Truly, we were a Christian family, the best we all knew how to be, but we missed the mark in many ways.

Once again, I am going to say, I am grateful for the foundations of faith and prayer. This gave me the strength and wisdom to reach out for more, notice more, and want more in my everyday life.

I loved hymns as a little child. Mother would often sing hymns as she worked, and I was in the children's choir. To this day, I remember the words of the hymn "Beautiful Savior."

> *"Beautiful Savior, King of creation, Son of God and Son of Man!*
>
> *Truly I'd love Thee, truly I'd serve thee, Light of my soul, my Joy, my Crown!*
>
> *Fair are the meadows, Fair are the woodland, robed in flow'rs of blooming spring:*
>
> *Jesus is fairer, Jesus is purer; He makes our sorr'wing spirit sing.*
>
> *Fair is the sunshine, Fair is the moonlight, bright the sparkling stars on high:*
>
> *Jesus shines brighter, Jesus shines purer, than all the angels in the sky.*

> *Beautiful Savior, Lord of the nations, Son of God and Son of Man,*
>
> *Glory and honor, Praise, adoration, now and forever more be Thine!"*

I loved singing that song as a nine-year-old and loved knowing the words, yet as an adult when we sang it in church, the words meant so much more. The song has spiritual power and is truly a form of prayer for me as many other hymns and wonderful songs are. Over the years, I became acquainted with contemporary songs of the 1980s, which are basic songs I sang as a prayer. Songs like, "Lord, I Lift Your Name on High" sung by the Maranatha Singers. The words help me to praise God and recognize how grateful I am to have Him in my life, especially at times like this.

I also love the lyrics of "I Love You, Lord" written by Laurie Klein. In a flash, these songs can be on my tongue as an intimate prayer, expanding my prayer life from the rote prayers of my youth to contemporary prayers of song and then conversations with God as if He were present in my room or car.

My prayer life grew in a subtle way, but I believe God was interacting with me and I was responding back to Him in the way I knew how to interact. Prayers of song grew as a part of my life even in my college years. When I was alone in the dorm on a Friday night, I would sing the liturgy from a Lutheran worship service or open my hymnal and sing a song. Such times filled my heart with peace, and I was never sad about not being out with my roommate. In fact, I went once to a frat party with a date and it was awful. I hated seeing the over-drinking and public displays of affection. I would rather sing, read a prayer, and rest than be a part of such behavior. I don't believe I was a prude; rather, it was the rhythm of my heart from a young age.

Throughout college, people made fun of me for getting up early on Sunday and walking to church or taking a bus. Their comments didn't negatively affect me because I was going where I really wanted to be. Sunday worship was a part of my life's rhythm, and it fed my soul. But when it became dry and lifeless for me, I moved on to another place to worship. It was just that simple. In fact, that is what happened with our family the year before John's grand mal seizure. Singing and speaking Lutheran liturgy was becoming stale for me, so we joined a local Presbyterian church looking for a fresh movement of the Spirit and a youth group for my son. I listened to what was happening within me and followed that nudging.

I am so glad we made the change. Our new congregation was such a blessing to us in our time of need—it was a fresh spiritual experience for us in the time leading up to the most dramatic season of our lives. The new congregation introduced our children to Westminster Woods campground, where their faith in the Lord Jesus took off. And the kids' Wednesday program and youth group gave them Christian friends for life. I also met wonderful friends whom I grew with and prayed with during my years of grieving. And I had a pastor who was so helpful for me in growing in the Lord. Thank you, Pastor Phil!

I will never forget our weekly meetings reading *The Practice of the Presence of God*, a collection of teachings written by Brother Lawrence, a seventeenth-century Carmelite friar. I still think about and talk about the ways Brother Lawrence approached life activities as a worship unto the Lord. When he peeled potatoes for the dinner meal, mundane task that it was, his mind was doing it as worship unto the Lord to bless his brothers in the monastery. When tasks are mundane, lifeless, boring, or very difficult, I have turned them into worship unto the Lord or a prayer to help me with the task.

Over the years, I have come to recognize that prayer is a rhythm of life, expressed sometimes in song, sometimes in reading a book, sometimes by doing a mundane or difficult task unto the Lord, sometimes in reading a prayer or *Guidepost* magazine, sometimes in saying a daily prayer or crying out to the Lord in need or anguish. Prayer is so much more than I was ever taught, yet I am grateful for the foundation of prayer

CHAPTER 7: FRAMEWORK OF PRAYER

I stood on to reach up to the new framework of prayer that developed around me by the grace of God and with the help of others.

I cannot finish this chapter without dwelling on the door in the center of the north wall of prayer for a moment. North makes me think of statements like "true north," like having a compass that points northward. The north wall faces "true north" for me, the location where the needle of my compass pointed, in the direction of the Lord. I have also said that I have a Geiger counter within me, one that beeps when I am heading in the direction of buried treasure. The more it beats and the faster it beats, the closer I am to the Lord's will and way. That beeping feels good and right. It tells me I am pleasing God, so keep going. And when I have reached that perfect location where God has led me, my Geiger counter beeps fast and makes me smile.

The "true north" door has been opening more over the years, until it was opened wide for the continual presence of Jesus in my heart, mind, and soul. He has sent into me the Holy Spirit, who is my Geiger counter, leading me to my purpose and to deeper love of the Lord. Writing this has brought forth another song that was an important part of this journey: "Jesus, name above all names, Beautiful Savior, glorious Lord," The lyrics talk about Jesus present, Emmanuel, and that He is the Living Word and our Redeemer. Singing the words of that song brought peace to my soul.

This presence led to the building of the sound roof above our home, the roof that was and is continually reaching up to the Heavens for more of Him in, around, and over our lives, healing us and maturing us more into His likeness. At this point, we will step into the third season I am writing about. The season of "Alive in Christ." As Christ held a greater presence in our home, He led us, permeated us, matured us, and indeed, began to heal us. I look forward to the writing of the final section of this book describing the roof of our home. Read on, dear ones.

Reflection Time

Think about your prayer life as a youngster. What prayers did you learn? What did they mean to you?

_____
_____
_____

Remember, prayer is talking with the Lord, just like you would talk to someone you know and love. Has prayer evolved for you, or are you still relying on memorized prayers? Are you ready for them to grow and evolve?

_____
_____
_____

Are you making time to pray outside of Sunday worship? Why or why not?

_____
_____
_____

Prayer Time

Now is the time to pray. Draw close to God with your thoughts about your life growing up, as an adult, and currently. Ask for help if you need to ask. He is a breath away from you.

Chapter 8

Cornerstone of My Framework
Surrender

"And coming to Him as to a living stone which has been rejected by men, but is choice and precious in the sight of God, you also, as living stones, are being built up as a spiritual house for a holy priesthood, to offer up spiritual sacrifices acceptable to God through Jesus Christ. For this is contained in scripture: 'Behold I lay in Zion a cornerstone, and he who believe in Him will not be disappointed.'"

— 1 Peter 2:4-8

"And He said to all, 'If anyone would come after me, let him deny himself and take up his cross daily and follow me."

— Luke 9:23

For much of my life, I was in control. As a child, I was in control of keeping my part of my room in order. I was in control of doing well in school. I was helpful in our home as needed. I was in control of learning to play an instrument. That control kept me at a distance emotionally from a lot of people, including the children in my classroom and neighborhood.

Being in control, organized, disciplined, and working hard helped me succeed in high school and college. These traits led to a life where I made things happen around me. I was often chosen to lead, and I was efficient and effective. Such a life made me a good teacher.

But when my family was in crisis, I could not handle it all. I was without my helpmate and often had no clue how to move forward. That was when I began to learn to surrender to the Lord's plan, provision, and way.

Earlier, I wrote about the way God surprised us during the final week of John's life when there were two gaps in our meal schedule. Those two days were the day John died and his funeral. Many stepped in to provide an abundance of food, more than we could use in those two days.

God's provision for finances was made clear when I didn't know anything about Social Security survivor benefits that the children and I were eligible for. Our financial picture was okay, but with the extra income from Supplemental Security Income (SSI), we were able to move forward in financial peace.

Slowly, I began to let go of the reins and gave God more and more control. Little by little, I discovered places where He wanted to provide or show me the way. As I surrendered, He led, and eventually God led me to full-time service in parish ministry. As I let go, I discovered my heart had desired to serve in the church from a young age. It didn't seem possible because in my faith tradition, women could only be teachers, and private schools didn't pay enough for me to support myself.

Over time, I began to say, "More of you, Lord, less of me." This surrender mantra, along with, "Let go and let God," were at the forefront of my mind for many years. It was not easy to parent three young children who became teens all at the same time. It was not easy to teach, care for our home and yard, and be an active part of a church. It was not easy to balance the tasks of life and friendship, but with God, we did it.

Surrender means letting go of control, and that was not easy for me. I am a leader, a take charge person, and letting go and allowing the unknown solution to come to me was often excruciatingly painful. But my life changed greatly as I continued to surrender situations that were out of my control to the Lord, finally letting go of my secure life as a teacher.

I sensed a call to parish ministry, which was confirmed when I was introduced to Rev. Dr. Brad Long at a prayer event in Southern California. Brad was the new leader of Presbyterian Renewal Ministries International, a ministry I had become involved in as I sought to bring more of the Lord into my life. Brad had recently accepted God's call to lead the ministry. It was exciting to meet him and hear him speak, teaching us and sharing his prior ministry in Taiwan. Late Saturday afternoon of the retreat, Brad moved around the room praying over everyone. When he laid his hand on my head, his prophetic message confirmed my call to ministry. At that point, Brad did not know me or anything about my life. Yet he confirmed what I had been sensing for some time.

This event took place in the mountains between Southern California and Central California in a campground at Lake Castaic in May 1990. As I walked out, I looked out over the valley below to the east. It was filled with small, yellow flowers—a sign of the many people I would impact in my future ministry, and it has indeed come to fruition during my twenty-five years of ordained ministry.

I left the mountain prepared to let go of my career in public education to teach God's Word in an entirely different setting. From that day forward, I surrendered completely to God's plan. He revealed the school I would attend, provided someone to rent our home for a year as I tested the seminary waters, and provided just the right home for us in the Pasadena area near where I would attend school.

In January 1993, I entered Fuller Theological Seminary to begin the new season of my life. A forty-five-year-old widowed seminary student with two high school daughters! What was God thinking? We had to proceed with God leading the way, all the way!

I surrendered my studies to the Lord and asked Him to show me the way. I felt a little out of place since I was forty-five and most of the students were in their late twenties. Quickly, I met the few older students and befriended many of the younger guys with whom I would spend much of the next three years in study, fellowship, and praying.

One summer, I was taking a five-week intensive class on the first five books of the Bible. This class was overwhelming because we were studying a book of the Bible per week and had a mid-term in week three. It was more than my brain could absorb. As I studied, I decided to memorize half of the material plus a little more. A short article that was part of our assignment was only available in the library. I had chosen to skip it and focus on what I thought was important. I was taking a walk before heading to Pasadena to take the exam, and I prayed as I walked. In response, God directed me to leave early to read the article in the library. I did so.

The final essay question, which was worth the most points, was about the article. Those who had not read the article missed all those points and ended up with low scores on the exam. Surrendering to the Lord, listening to His direction, allowed me to pass that exam. I saw how much God cares about everything, even one exam question.

In January of my final year, it became clear I would not have enough money to complete the year without help. I prayed about my need as I kept my need to myself and the Lord. One morning, I woke remembering my dream from that night. I saw white envelopes falling from the sky. I was puzzled, but soon I began receiving checks in the mail in white envelopes, including refunds I didn't know would come, a church deciding to pay for my books, and friends who decided to bless me. All of this was totally unexpected. People handed me envelopes with cash, and in the final month, the deacons of my internship church surprised me with a $1,000 check to pay my rent. I never asked anyone for help. I merely prayed to the Lord. I shared the miracles with the small group I was in called Women of the Spirit, and we all rejoiced in the blessing and provision of the Lord helping me finish seminary as planned.

Surrender has become my way of life. As provision was evident, I became more and more confident in God's plan and God's way. They were always superior to what I wanted. Letting go and letting God is a tremendously difficult life pattern, one I believe God desires for us all.

If letting go and letting God is new to you, try asking God what His plan is for something in your life and listening to God's response. Offer your needs to the Lord and see what He will do for you.

Reflection Time

Can you remember a time when you let go and let God show you the way or make the provisions? If so, write about such a time or write about your struggle with letting go.

_____
_____
_____

Surrendering one's life to the Lord's purpose and plan is a major challenge but so worth it. Write about how you feel thinking about this. What would you let go and why?

_____
_____
_____

Prayer Time

Ask God about what you might surrender to His plan. Offer something you are struggling with to God and ask for His provision and/or clarity about the direction He would have you go.

Season 3

Rooftop
Reaching to the Heavenlies

Rooftop Introduction—The Importance of the Rooftop

"Don't you know that you yourselves are God's temple (sanctuary) and God's Spirit lives in you? If anyone destroys God's temple (sanctuary), God will destroy him; for God's temple (sanctuary) is sacred and you are that temple (sanctuary)."

— 1 Corinthians 3:16-17

Now that we have looked at the foundation and framework of my home, let us look at the placement of the roof, which is where my home becomes a sanctuary for the presence of the Lord. It is a place where I go for respite from the world's challenges to regroup, unite, heal, and reach up to the Heavenlies. The Foundation was built securely by my family, the solid place on which we stand. The Framework was put into place as John and I took hold of the foundational pieces and built walls around our family, walls of security and strength. And now we explore the Roof of our family. It was our place of security, of reaching upward to the Lord for leadership, healing, vision, and future. As we stood on the basics built by my family, we were wrapped with walls of family, financial strength, friends, and prayer, forming a solid base for raising the rooftop and reaching higher and higher to greater places we could never have reached on our own.

In this season, the concept of God's Kingdom on Earth was revealed. As a daughter of the King of Kings and Lord of Lords, I sat at His feet for hours to discover what my life and the lives of my children meant. As I sought the Lord, I discovered the importance of intimacy with God in surprising and sometimes simple ways. My heart and soul were healed through prayer, devotion, and love of others. Life as I knew it was being transformed through the presence of the Triune God: Father, Son, and Holy Spirit. I allowed their hands, God's Word, the faithfulness of others, and my surrender to take hold, bringing forth the Transformation that only God can do.

In the midst of the Healing and Transformation, I began to gain greater and greater glimpses of God's call. The first phase of my call was to parish ministry and included letting go of my secure teaching career to learn to teach within congregations and ministries. In this current era of my life, my calling to mentor, coach, teach, preach, and pray with people throughout the world is evolving. My new calling is to help usher in a new movement of bringing the Lord into the lives of people who have been attending church for years but never knew they could have an intimate relationship with God. So many believers and even pastors follow paths of their own choosing, rather than listening to and following the voice of the Lord. My passion expands to helping Christian widows reach for the embrace of the Lord during their grieving season. Several people, including widows, have been healed as they learned and experienced the presence of the Lord. My mentorship helps women discover their identity in the Lord and His purpose for their Kingdom lives. As they learn to hear the "still small voice" and to obey it at all costs, life transformation begins to happen. How glorious it is to see how God is able to heal and bring transformation into their lives.

In this final season of my book, you will see some of the journey God took me on to climb out of grief into a transformed life of helping others seek God. In doing so, I have seen the message found in Romans 8:28, "And we know that in all things God works for the good of those who love Him, who have been called according to His purpose" proven true. Indeed, in this third season of my life, God has been diligent in redeeming the tremendous loss of my husband and my children's father. Of course, God didn't bring John back to life, but He has taken each of our lives and healed, wooed, and transformed us to be more in His likeness so we might have a greater Kingdom impact on Earth.

We will begin by examining what Kingdom on Earth means to us. Next, I will talk about having intimacy with God, and what my journey of learning about God, the Son, and the Holy Spirit, seeking, heart healing over the loss, and so much more that was hidden in my heart and soul was like. Then I will talk about God's Transformation and what it might look like. And finally, we will look at listening to God's call to our life's purpose, a purpose He has for each of us. This is a journey inward to find a healthier and more whole way to reach out to others to help them heal, worship, and find their purpose. This journey inevitably leads to becoming a Living Sanctuary of the Lord. Let's get moving on the journey!

Reflection Time

What loss has you stuck? Is it the loss of a marriage, a spouse, a child, a career/job, a home, your health, or some other life-interrupting crisis? Reflect on and write what has you stuck and what steps forward you will make.

_____

_____

_____

Have you been seeking the Lord to learn His way of redeeming your life for the good of the Kingdom? Write about the ways you seek the Lord on a daily basis.

_____

_____

_____

Are you ready for a fresh new journey with God? What will it look like?

_____
_____
_____

Prayer Time

Ask God for clarity about your loss and how He wants you to focus on redemption. Pray about how this might be a blessing to others. Seeking God is a surrendered way; He does have a plan.

Chapter 9

Experiencing the Lord

"And he said, 'My presence will go with you, and I will give you rest."
— Exodus 33:14

God began pressing into my life in several unique and wonderful ways, signaling that He was present as we navigated these tough years. In this chapter, I will look at three of the most memorable encounters I had with the Lord. The first happened on the airplane when my children and I returned to California from Michigan as John lay in the intensive care unit of a Sacramento hospital.

Warm Oil Poured Over My Head

"He poured some of the anointing oil on Aaron's head
and anointed him to consecrate him."
— Leviticus 8:12

"Then the Lord said, 'Rise and anoint him; this is the one.' So, Samuel took the horn of oil and anointed him in the presence of his brothers, and from that day on, the Spirit of the Lord came powerfully upon David."
— 1 Samuel 16:12b-13a

In August of 1986, we flew back to California on last-minute tickets that left my children scattered about the airplane's cabin. I sat near the back to keep an eye on them. I was seated with two strangers, which gave me time alone in my head. I did not like flying in those days, and I always prayed during takeoff and descent. That day I *prayed* and continued to pray.

The two days between finding out John was in the hospital and boarding the plane had been exhausting and actually seemed like a week. I laid my head back on the headrest and began to pray, "Lord, help me; help John; show us a way!" As we traveled along, I felt the presence of the Lord come upon me. Then I began to feel something like warm oil being poured over my head. Suddenly, I remembered the biblical story of the oil poured over Aaron's head as described in Psalm 133:2-3: "It is like precious oil poured on the head running down on the beard, running down on Aaron's beard, down on the collar of his robe. It is as if the dew of Hermon were falling on Mt. Zion. For there the Lord bestows His blessing, even life forevermore." That oil was warm and comforting. I knew the Lord's hand was somehow guiding this situation and my life. And I felt peace beyond all understanding the rest of the flight.

As we climbed off the plane in Sacramento, I had a greater sense of the presence of God. We greeted our friends, Pat, Karen, and their spouses, and stepped into a tremendously challenging situation. Yet I was given the clear knowledge that God was present and would be with us. The warm oil was a new calling—a calling to walk with God into life as it would become.

Hearing the Voice

"And your ears shall hear a Word behind you, saying, 'This is the way, walk in it, when you turn to the right or when you turn to the left.'"

— Isaiah 30:21

During John's final year, my hunger for more of the Lord entered my life in ways I never knew possible. In the late evening hours, John would fall asleep in his recliner as I headed upstairs for some me time—time to shower, get ready for bed and the next day, and spend time with a stack of books. My goal each night was to read one chapter from each of the books I had stacked on the nightstand and then read from my Bible. Often when I took John to a doctor's appointment or visited him in the hospital, I would stop at a Christian bookstore for more reading material. The majority of the books were about the Holy Spirit.

When I was a child, I rarely heard anything in the Lutheran churches we attended about the Holy Spirit except at the end of worship when the pastor would make the sign of the cross and say, "In the name of the Father, the Son, and the Holy Ghost." As a child in the 1950s, I thought, "Who wants to know anything about a ghost?" And since the pastor never preached on this ghost, I had let that topic lie dormant until this final year of John's life.

In this new season I faced, I began to think more deeply about the Holy Ghost or Holy Spirit. My thirst for knowledge about the third person of the Trinity was unquenchable. I purchased many books about the Holy Spirit (I imagine some were heresy!) to try to satisfy my parched soul. As I read, studied, and prayed, my new life in the Lord grew. Yet I was not completely satisfied, so I continued to search for more and more.

One evening when I was alone in our bedroom, I heard a voice speak to me. It was clear it was not from my thoughts or from John, who was asleep downstairs. I looked around asking, "Who said that?" I got no answer, but the message welled up inside my soul. "Don't let your son drown." What in the world did that mean? I ran downstairs to talk with John about this unique, for me, experience.

We were puzzled: Who had spoken? What did the message mean? What should we do about the message?

First, I must say I did not know then that God still speaks to us today. I thought that was just for people in the Bible. If our pastors ever said anything about God speaking to us, I must have been daydreaming and missed the message. But in that moment, that night, someone was clearly speaking to me from a different realm. I had no idea what was happening.

If it were God, how were we to protect our son? After all, we didn't live near water and had a very small above the ground backyard pool—it was only eighteen inches deep. All we could do at the moment was tuck the message away and take extra precautions with our son around pools.

The greatest revelation was Heaven breaking through to my bedroom. I evidently heard the voice of God offering a word of caution. And from that day forward, I began to witness God sending me messages in other ways. I noticed many of my prayers being answered, events that were truly not coincidences, and a growing strength within me no matter what direction my life turned.

God's hand was clearly with our family during this intense time of decline and loss. He provided a doctor to tell us about John's health, a wonderful, helpful oncologist, and support for our family through Stephen Ministers and neighbors. Our family was provided with meals for two solid months and a freezer full of leftovers for those days when we just could do nothing more.

God's voice and God's nudges became more apparent in my daily way of life. My surrendered life sought His lead, His voice, and His answers to challenges in scriptures, a sermon, or a song. That voice I heard that evening, when the warning message was to watch out for the safety of my son, was the first time I became aware of the voice of the Lord reaching through the thin veil between Heaven and earth. It was challenging me to listen to the still small voice. This incident was significant for my intimate journey with the Lord. And years later, I recognized the warning was not about drowning in water, but a warning to be sure my son would not drown in sorrow over the death of his dad. For many years, I pondered those words because they seemed so random to me, yet the weight of them was heavy on my mind. They were a preparation to pray for him, which I did. Those prayers and the prayers of my Women of the Spirit helped him through many years of sorrow into becoming a productive business owner, husband, father, and missionary. I am so grateful for the warning.

Mantle of the Lord

"So, Elijah went from there and found Elisha, son of Shaphat. He was plowing with twelve yoke of oxen, and he himself was driving the twelfth pair. Elijah went up to him and threw his mantle around him. Elisha then left his oxen and ran after Elijah. 'Let me kiss my father and mother goodbye,' he said, 'and then I will come with you.' 'Go back,' Elijah replied. 'What have I done to you?' So, Elisha left him and went back. He took his yoke of oxen and slaughtered them. He burned the plowing equipment to cook the meat and gave it to the people, and they ate. Then he set out to follow Elijah and became his servant."

— 1 Kings 19:19-21

After John died, I continued to seek people who understood God in the way I was learning to understand. God brought a woman into my life at a church retreat who also wanted more of God in her life. We grew in prayer and friendship. One fall, we discovered a Lutheran conference on the Holy Spirit being held in Minneapolis, Minnesota. We made arrangements for our children and headed to the event. Oh, how exciting it was for me to see several hundred Lutherans with their hands held high in worship of our Lord. I loved the singing and teaching. I had finally found a whole room full of people who had learned to know Jesus as I had been learning.

As we sat together waiting for the session to begin on Saturday morning, I felt a tap on my left shoulder. I looked to the left and over my shoulder, but no one was there. Hmm. I looked to the right to see if someone were spoofing me and reaching across my back to tap me. Nope. No one there either. Then I asked my friend if she had tapped me. "No." As I sat wondering what had happened—had I imagined it? No, it felt real—I felt the touch again. This time it was like an invisible mantle was placed over my shoulders—the mantle of the Lord was placed on me. It was a sign of God taking my load and placing His light mantle on my shoulders. This spiritual experience began my journey toward ordination and parish ministry. And indeed, it was a journey. In retrospect, it was a journey that had been coming for years, but now my path was clear as I pressed into what God was doing in my life.

These three breakthroughs from Heaven over a four-year period were significant to my movement forward in my relationship with the Lord. I heard the voice of the Lord, and I learned that He speaks to us today. I learned the importance of paying attention to the voice, the nudges, and the clear revelations that come to my mind. Next, I was made aware of the presence of God in the warm oil poured over me in my prayer time on the plane. It was not real oil, yet a tangible presence of God that helped me know He was with me in that crisis and in the days forward. Then the placing of the mantle on my shoulders revealed to me His willingness to trade my heavy burdens for His light mantle. He would carry the weight I would endure, lead the way, and provide as I needed if I would just continually turn to Him.

I pray that you will see these three incidents in my life as a reminder to you that God is present always, He is there for you, and He is speaking to you continually. Your relationship and experiences will certainly be different and unique to you and your circumstances. Nonetheless, they will valuable to you as you grow in your journey with Him.

Reflection Time

Have you had a surprising encounter with the Lord or had anything happen that puzzled you like the oil, the voice, or the tap?

_____
_____
_____

If so, do you understand what this encounter was about? Write what you think God is telling you.

_____
_____
_____

If you have not noticed such an encounter, begin to pay closer attention to your life and ways God may be attempting to get your attention.

I believe God was calling me closer and preparing me for greater intimacy with Him for my future call. Did you know that the Lord wants to interact with us? He sends the Holy Spirit to challenge us, encourage us, enlighten us, or get our attention. Watch, ask, and listen. He is present.

Prayer Time

Ask the Lord to reveal His presence in your life. Ask Him to show you where He tried to get your attention and you missed it. Ask for more connections and a closer relationship with Him. Let it begin.

Chapter 10
Rooftop–The Revelation

"Now Moses was tending the flock of Jethro, his father-in-law, the priest of Midian, and he led the flock to the far side of the wilderness and came to Horeb, the mountain of God. There the angel of the Lord appeared to him in the flames of fire from within a bush. Moses saw that though the bush was on fire it did not burn up. So Moses thought, 'I will go over and see this strange sight—why the bush does not burn up.' When the Lord saw that he had gone over to look, God called to him from within the bush, 'Moses! Moses!' And Moses said, 'Here I am.' 'Do not come any closer,' God said. 'Take off your sandals, for the place where you are standing is holy ground.'"

— Exodus 3:1-5

The Burning Bush

While reading about the Holy Spirit, I was asked to lead the women's retreat for our Lutheran congregation. The topic was the Holy Spirit. I didn't know much about this topic, yet I knew more than all of the other women at the retreat. One of the women was a neighbor of mine who was greatly impacted by what I taught at that retreat. One day in the fall of 1987, just five months after John's death, she called to invite me to attend a charismatic prayer group being held at a neighbor's home. I agreed to attend with her, hoping to learn more about the Holy Spirit through these people.

The evening began with a welcome and opening prayer followed by the singing of several Marantha songs (contemporary worship songs). I felt comfortable in that group even though it was a different expression of faith from mine because the group focused on Jesus and prayer. Once the singing was finished, the leader, Charley, announced a change in the normal routine. He had us break into five different groups of four people to pray for each other. My group was in the living room with Charley, his assistant Paul, and the friend who brought me to the session to pray for me as the group was aware of my recent widowhood.

The men pulled up a dining room chair and asked me to sit in it as they stood in front of me to pray. My friend sat on the floor next to me. Charley asked how they could pray for me. I said, "I need the Lord to show me how to raise my children on my own." They were nine, twelve, and fourteen then.

Charley and Paul stood in front of me with their hands lifted in front of my head, but not touching me. Charley began the prayer, and then Paul joined in. I sat in the wooden chair, thinking the prayer was nice, when suddenly a hand (not theirs) touched my forehead, pushing my head backward. Tears welled up and began to run down my cheeks, and I felt a powerful presence within my heart. I didn't hear a voice other than their prayers. When they stopped praying, they merely stood before me with their hands lifted in front of me waiting on the Lord.

I had never experienced anything like this. It felt wonderful, yet I didn't know what to do. Soon I wondered, *What is happening and when will it be over?* I opened my eyes a bit and saw the ceiling was filled with flames—more tears, more peace, more of Him. I gazed at those flames, not burning the house, for several minutes, soaking in the refining fire of the Spirit of God into my heart and mind. Finally, my neck grew tired from leaning backward, so I sat upright. Charley said, "What just happened?" They had not seen the flames, nor had my friend, but they believed that God was present and would be leading me as He had led

CHAPTER 10: ROOFTOP—THE REVELATION 117

Moses and the Israelites in the wilderness. The men hugged me and left to see if they were needed elsewhere.

My friend and I hugged and talked, then decided to leave. Once I was home, I climbed into bed wondering what had happened and what it would mean for my life. I had arrived at the meeting so innocent. And I left enlightened about the Lord in new and exciting ways, growing in wonderment of God and His ways.

The following day was a normal school day until after the children had gone to bed. Then I lit a candle in the master bathroom, turned out the light, closed the door, filled up the tub with hot water and bubble bath, then climbed in to soak away the day's stress. For years, I had relaxed in the tub after school to prepare myself to make dinner and participate in family activities. But after John's death, I had switched that soaking time to later in the evening, after the children were sleeping so I could have time alone with God.

I settled into the tub, relaxing and thinking about the many unique experiences I had been having: the oil over my head on the airplane, hearing the voice in the evening warning us about not letting our son drown, and now the flames. My thoughts included worship time, the flames, the tears, and once again, the assurance of God's presence in my life, a life that by all outward appearances was a disaster. No husband, no dad for my children—what would life look like without John. He had been the glue for us. Yet God was continually reminding me that He would not leave me or forsake me. He would be with me in this journey no matter what.

Soon I began to speak to the Lord. "Lord, I am not sure what happened to me or what it means. I heard people speaking in a language I do not know. I just want to pray the best I am able. Help me to know how to pray to you and hear you." Then I began singing a praise song, but it was not in a language I knew or understood. Yet I knew what I was singing because it was a song I knew well. It was God's answer to my prayer in a way I didn't ask for, yet one that answered my request. My prayer language began to develop from that day forward. When I didn't know how to pray, the Spirit prayed in ways my limited mind didn't know to request.

In the following days, people would greet me by saying, "You must have a boyfriend." I guess I had a continual smile on my face. They thought it was something earthly like a new man in my life. I answered, "Yes, I do, but not one like you would think." I was falling in love with Jesus!

Soon, I began to have regular appointments with the Lord at about two in the morning. I would awake; God would speak, teach, or answer a concern; then I would go back to sleep, awakening fully rested in the morning. One night, I asked, "Why do you wake me at 2 a.m. to talk, Lord?" His answer makes me smile today. "That is when I can have your full attention." So true, between teaching, caring for a home, laundry, meals, and raising three children, my days were full. Yet I needed God's guidance. His answers in the middle of the night were just what I needed. Soon, I began to rely on Him for guidance, provision, and wisdom. The way I looked at life began to change, and my circle of friends began to grow as God brought people into my life who wanted more of what I was experiencing with God.

Often, friends would ask, "What is going on in your life?" I learned it was safe to share my spiritual experiences with those who asked. So, I saved those treasures for those who would hear, much like Jesus telling parables to the masses and knowing people who had ears to hear would fully understand the message He was imparting. I didn't use parables, but I learned to withhold my stories until someone asked, "What is going on in your life?" Those friends would be hungry for more of the Lord and would attend the prayer meeting with me. How exciting it was to see others come to know the Lord as I was experiencing God.

CHAPTER 10: ROOFTOP—THE REVELATION

A New Way of Life

"Therefore, if anyone is in Christ, the new creation has come. The old has gone, the new is here!"

— 2 Corinthians 5:17

Evidence of the supernatural in God's way of speaking to me included the flames on the ceiling, the new people wanting to join me in this crazy journey, the early morning conversations, the oil poured over my head, and the mantle of the Lord. Truly God was in the midst of turning my life toward Him and away from my old ways. This journey was unique, different from that of anyone I have ever met, a journey that called and equipped me to touch lives in many churches, ministries, and now as I develop Joyful Kingdom Living. This is where we meet, at the threshold of life grounded in the Lord and His ways. It has been years since those first experiences, yet they have never stopped. I continue to have daily encounters with the Lord. It is a way of life for me. The Lord and I interact every morning and often throughout the day. It is the way He would love for us all to have a relationship with Him in His Kingdom on Earth.

I freely admit my faith journey was different as a child from anyone else's I knew in Sunday School. I was serious about memorizing the books of the Bible as a seven-year-old. I was serious about learning the songs in children's choir like "Beautiful Savior." I was serious about the material in our confirmation classes and Luther's Catechism. I was serious about helping at Vacation Bible School as a high schooler and taking a leadership role in our youth group. I was serious about attending worship throughout my life. And I was serious about singing the liturgy and praying rote prayers in my private time. It drew me close to God. That was truly out of the norm for anyone I knew. But it was me, the me who, as an adult, stepped into a new realm of relationship with the Lord by following the Holy Spirit.

God showed me that He was pleased with my commitment, yet He wanted me to know there was more. There was more to God than I learned in Sunday School, Vacation Bible School, church, or youth group. He was becoming my teacher, my counselor, my lover, and my healer. He taught me about things no one ever mentioned anywhere I had been, and I had to search for others who were learning as I have learned.

The good news is you don't have to seek for as long as I had to seek. You don't have to go through thirty-five-plus years of seeking and growing through so many things like I did. I am willing to share what I have experienced and what I know about the Lord. This new era of my life is focused on teaching about the Triune God, the Kingdom of God on the earth, the ministry of Jesus, and the work of the Holy Spirit. If you want to learn more, experience the presence of God, hear the voice of the Lord, and all that He has for you, just reach out your hand and lead the way.

"You were taught, with regard to your former way of life, to put off your old self, which is being corrupted by its deceitful desires; to be made new in the attitude of your minds; and to put on the new self, created to be like God in true righteousness and holiness."

— Ephesians 4:22-24

Reflection Time

I have never met another person who has had a burning bush experience like I experienced, but that doesn't mean He doesn't interact with people in other ways. Has He interacted with you in a unique way others haven't talked about? If so, write about it.

_____

_____

_____

CHAPTER 10: ROOFTOP—THE REVELATION

If not, ask Him to come close to you in a way that draws your attention to Him.

Does this burning bush encounter challenge your way of thinking about the Lord? Does it make you uncomfortable? If so, why?

_____
_____
_____

My saying yes and just going along with what the Lord was doing was new and foreign to me every step of the way. Are you willing and ready to follow this path?

_____
_____
_____

Do you want to know God's will and follow God's lead in some challenging situation you are in right now? He can lead you. Seek Him and pay attention to new thoughts and new ways to move forward.

Prayer Time

Ask God to reveal Himself to you in a way you are sure is Him. Ask Him to make His voice clear to you. Thank Him for wanting to be close to us and for you wanting to be close to Him.

Chapter 11

Looking Inward and Reaching Upward

"You will know the truth, and the truth will set you free."
— John 8:32

Bondage Breaker

The more I read, the more I prayed, the more I saw deep pain within me and patterns of living that were not pleasing the Lord. One way I became more aware of my brokenness and sin was attending conferences where pastors and teachers revealed the truths of a sinful life and how my and my parents' pain influenced my life, holding me back from a fuller relationship with the Lord and others.

One summer, a man named Dr. Neil T. Anderson offered a five-evening conference called "The Bondage Breaker" at a local church. Anderson was a professor at Talbot School of Theology in Southern California in the practical theology department. I was intrigued by the article in the *Vacaville Reporter* announcing the conference and the concepts he would be teaching. It seemed to be what I needed that summer, so I enrolled. I was not disappointed.

Anderson spoke about generational patterns and sins we inherit, in addition to ways we open ourselves up to the work of dark spirits to have their way in our lives. The stories from his personal experiences held me captive. After the conference, I did a serious study of my family origins and my own life choices that had created my way of life and which of them had hindered my close walk with the Lord.

I created a genogram of my family going back four generations. On this map, one can see the patterns of sin or illness that wind through a family. I was able to see the trail of cancer, miscarriages, early deaths, broken marriages, and ways of living. Anderson instructed us to claim victory over our family lines by taking an invisible pair of scissors to cut away the old and then claim wholeness in the family line from us forward. Over and over, I prayed for my family and myself, praying that the old ways that had been revealed would no longer limit me, my children, and my children's children for a thousand generations. In place of the old ways, we were to pray the wholeness and love of Jesus into all of the crevices of our lives that were empty of the darkness and ready for new filling. Slowly, I began to see my life change for the better. As my life changed, I interacted with others differently at home, at work, in my community, and at church. I began to have a renewed mind and new, healthier patterns.

I want to thank Dr. Anderson for being the first person to teach me about these patterns in the lives of believers that hold them captive. As I read and worked through his workbook *The Bondage Breaker* with Jesus' help and guidance, I found light in the dark corners and cervices of my inner soul. From there, I read Dr. Anderson's books *Victory Over the Darkness* and *The Steps to Freedom in Christ*. I highly recommend this material, which is ingrained with prayer and scripture. I continue to use many of the principles Dr. Anderson taught in the inner healing ministry I do with people who cross my path.

It was evident that God was drawing me to teachers and books that would bring forth greater revelation about how to live a life in Christ and for His purposes. Year by year, I discovered ministries, books, workshops, and conferences where I learned more and more about the healing power of Christ and the work of the Holy Spirit.

Inner Healing

> *"If we confess our sins, He is faithful and just to forgive us our sins and to cleanse us from all unrighteousness."*
>
> — 1 John 1:9

In 1998, while I was in my first pastorate in El Centro, California, I became aware of a training program on inner healing and deliverance ministry through Presbyterian Renewal Ministries International (PRMI). Since I was an ordained Presbyterian pastor and part of PRMI, I opted to use my study leave to take the training. We took four trips to Black Mountain, North Carolina, for three days training on the weekend. We had twelve books to read, reflection papers to write, and many practice sessions. During this year of training, more and more brokenness within me was revealed as I read, wrote, prayed, and was prayed for by others in our classes. Encounters with God as I sought Him were increasing, along with visions and dreams that were clearly guiding my life.

The closer I got to God, the more I saw what was hidden within the dark recesses of my soul. One time, I remembered the "Get out of here, baby" tickle incident I spoke of earlier. My father's reaction had wounded me deeply. My father and I had been so much closer before it happened. He and I were much alike in our personality, both being introverts. We processed life inwardly, whereas my mother and sister were extroverts who processed life externally.

That inner hurt began to define my life from that day forward. I felt like a "nobody" and lost my confidence. Daddy was pretty silent in much of our life, so a verbal rejection countered a thousand words of affirmation from my mom. I had many inner healing sessions over this one-minute interaction. Daddy had forgotten it long ago; my soul had not.

I forgave Daddy for those words and felt somewhat better. Yet, this incident continued to crop up over the years. I forgave my sister for stealing the scene. I prayed about the self-definition of being a "nobody." Over and over, this scene would come forward, and the wound continued to fester as other rejections began to pile on top of this scene (Scene One). Soon I was living a life of pain, inadequacy, rejection, and isolation. I would strive for success at the expense of others so I could have my time in the limelight.

I prayed and forgave. Rocks and pebbles were tossed away from this huge pile of rejection. I had some freedom, but it was still there. One day recently, I was sitting with the Lord in the morning when He showed me an image of Him and me. I was face to face with Him, and He said, "Lonely." *Wow!* I thought. Then I saw from the moment of that one-minute interaction that troubled my entire life that I had felt lonely. That moment had cast a shadow over my entire life, limiting my relationships and robbing me of many potential successes.

Mind you, I had grown closer and closer to the Lord over the previous sixty years. I had released a lot of pain, rejection, sin, and life patterns, yet I knew something was still not right within me. I was very close to the Lord, yet I often awoke in the morning after John's death with an aching heart that undermined my morning.

I said, "Lord, I don't want loneliness to be part of my life any longer. I know you can fill that spot." In an instant, the Lord removed loneliness and replaced it with His joy and peace. Since that morning, my days are filled with alone time but not loneliness.

The peace, comfort, and joy of intimacy with God can lead us to freedom from that which lingers within, stealing and destroying the full life in the Lord that He wants for us. This is why I teach about inner healing and offer inner healing sessions. Drawing near to the Lord reveals what is in the way of drawing so close that we can hear words like, "Lonely," and know that God wants it gone from us.

Cleansing Streams

> *"I will not leave you orphans; I will come to you.... If anyone loves me, he will keep My word; and My Father will love him, and We will come to him and make Our home with him. He who does not love Me does not keep My words; and the word which you hear is not Mine but the Father's, who sent Me."*
>
> — John 14:18, 23-24

In the spring of 2011, I was part of a program called "Cleansing Streams." It, too, teaches about life patterns from which we can free ourselves. I had been attending a Sunday morning Cleansing Stream class that would prepare us for a day and a half conference in Los Angeles.

One morning around that time, when I stepped in the shower, I heard the word "Orphan." *Hmm?* I thought. *What is that about, Lord?* My parents were alive, I had three grown children, two married, and four grandsons. I have a sister, a multitude of cousins, aunts, and uncles. "I am not an orphan. Why did you say that?" I asked.

After I showered, I went to pick up my grandson and drove him an hour away to Glendale for preschool. I hung out in a local parking lot for two hours, waiting for him to finish his preschool session. You can imagine I spent the two hours talking to God and journaling about this word "orphan." As I wrote, the Lord revealed I had not emotionally bonded with my mom the way I should have as a baby. We had not become fully attached, which caused me pain in the form of going through life looking for the inner satisfaction of belonging to someone. John was in Heaven, my parents lived across the country, and I was disconnected from them emotionally.

"Thank you, God, for revealing this to me, but what do I do about it?" I asked. No answer came while I journaled, prayed, and waited. That night when the conference started, the leader announced, "We are changing things up tonight. If you have ever been to a Cleansing Streams weekend, you will notice that we will start with a new topic, 'The Orphan Spirit.'" The Cleansing Streams people had discovered many people live with the "Orphan Spirit" as I had, and it interferes with all of the other healing they hoped for us that weekend. Our amazing God wanted me to know I had lived as an orphan, opening me up for the orphan spirit, which robbed me of healthy connections and relationships. This revelation made it possible for me to seek healing prayer that night for what I might have not known I needed. The voice speaking, "Orphan" caused me to ponder my life all day prior to the Cleansing Streams retreat. That evening, I had the beginning of the breakthrough of the orphan spirit in control of my life. God is so good.

I was so grateful for intimacy with the Lord that evening and for the revelation He gave me of the major focus of the weekend for me. Not only does God want us to know Him personally, but He wants us free of that which binds us. That weekend, I was set free from the orphan spirit, and I am always on the lookout for ways it might want to creep back into my life.

Living in Increased Freedom

"So, if the Son sets you free, you will be free indeed."
— John 8:36

Looking in the rearview mirror of my life, I see the first sentence God spoke to me as I discovered the voice of God in my life. Then turning to today, as I stare through the wide front window of life, I see the millions of steps I have taken to draw close to Him. He has revealed so many things I have held on to with a death grip that had limited my life. In replacing everything He removed and healed, He has taken over more of my heart, mind, and soul.

In Mark 12:28-31, we see a man ask Jesus what the most important commandment is. Jesus' reply was, "Love the Lord your God with all of your heart, your mind, your soul, and your strength, and love your neighbor as yourself." That verse became a life verse for me in 2002 when I was working with a ministry for military wives. The director often quoted Mark, "Love your neighbor as yourself." I took it a step farther and made Christ's entire response the center post of my life.

I discovered finding the loving God with my heart, soul, mind, and strength was not something I could do on my own. I could strive, but all of the brokenness within me limited how much I could love the Lord, myself, and others. The scripture was in my heart. I continued to repeat it, and the more inner healing I found, the more I realized God was and is helping me to love Him with every part of me, my belongings, and my life. The more I am healed, the more I am able to love Him and want to love Him more. I am happy when I am alone with God, and I am happy to love, teach, and serve others. God so wants our love that He helps us love Him more by healing our broken ways if we let Him.

Reflection Time

Have you ever searched your inner soul for things that happened that you have not overcome? Now would be a good time to do so. Close your eyes, relax, and look deep into your soul for hurts and pains you have pushed aside. Ask God what is hidden if nothing comes forward. Then write about that memory. It would be good to now give it over to Jesus and be free.

Is there remaining pain in your heart over your family's struggles with marriage, finances, careers, or relationships? Once again, close your eyes and ask Jesus what is hidden there that you haven't thought about for a very long time. Do you feel pain when you think about it? If so, can you hand that hurt to Jesus and let Him have it? Be free. Write about this experience and how it feels to have let the pain go.

_____
_____
_____

Do you live in a negative environment or see yourself judging people? Are you a judging person, or do you feel judged? It hurts, doesn't it? Write about the situation. Offer it up to Jesus. Whether it is you doing the judging or you feel judged, it all needs to go away. Be free. Now write about the situation and how you feel at this moment.

_____
_____
_____

Many things may have come forward in the three different activities. You can daily journal about what you remember and release it to Jesus. Seeking a pastor or trustworthy person to pray with might help you, or you might seek out an inner healing minister.

Prayer Time

Ask God to show you what might be hidden within you that is holding you back. Ask Him to lead you to help or to heal you from the injuries. Ask God to help you live a solid, upright, steadfast life that is pleasing to Him.

Chapter 12
Rooftop-Spiritual Disciplines

"All Scripture is breathed out by God and profitable for teaching, for reproof, for correction, and for training in righteousness, that the man of God may be complete, equipped for every good work."

— 2 Timothy 3:16-17

In the early 1990s, I was introduced to the Christian writer Richard Foster, who was a Quaker theologian scholar, professor, and author. His life purpose was to help others develop and mature their walk with Jesus. The first book of his I read, actually devoured, is titled *Celebration of the Disciplines*. Since I had already been on the spiritual discipline journey for five years by then, it was natural for me to consume everything he wrote and begin to put it into practice.

Foster created three categories for the twelve spiritual disciplines he wrote about: inward, outward, and corporate. Many other authors have written about spiritual disciplines, describing other ways to focus on them in developing a personal relationship with the Lord. I happen to have met Dr. Foster and began to fervently practice most of the twelve he wrote about.

I am going to take the time to list the topics in those three categories before I move forward:

Inward: meditate, fasting, prayer, study

Outward: simplicity, solitude, submission, service

Corporate: confession, worship, guidance, celebration (fellowship)

I could write an entire book myself on these twelve categories, but I will share just one from each area so you might see their value for your personal spiritual growth. I recommend reading *Celebration of the Disciplines* and slowly beginning to incorporate these disciplines into your life. Just like it is difficult to go "cold turkey" (stop smoking) or run a marathon, so it is difficult to overwhelm your life with all twelve at once. More than likely, it will become a chore for you and one that becomes dry and pointless. The point of incorporating these disciplines in our lives is to draw us closer to intimacy with our Lord, not as a check-off list or a victory, but as a loving discipline to right our lives into a closer alignment with God's purpose and ways in our lives.

Worship had always been a part of my life from the womb. My father's family are all devout Lutherans, never missing worship and never missing the rote prayers that were part of worship or family life. When my parents married, my mother quickly became involved in the Lutheran Church, making it an important pattern of life. We never missed worship unless we were so sick we could not get out of bed. It was a life pattern passed down for generations, and fortunately, it continues to be so for my children and grandchildren.

As a teen, worshiping was a rhythm of life I took as my own. I loved being in worship, learning the songs in the hymnal along with the liturgy. In fact, I would find a church offering a special Lenten or Holy Week service if one was not being offered at my local church. For me, it was more than a ritual; it was a deep desire to be with God and God's people in such a holy way. Worship brought a peace within my soul, which I was not able to describe; nonetheless, it was there.

CHAPTER 12: ROOFTOP—SPIRITUAL DISCIPLINES 133

I remember driving into the country in East Lansing as a twenty-year-old to have a quiet place to pray aloud and sing a song or a hymn. It was a need and a pure rhythm of my life. So, when Foster described it as a spiritual discipline, I could see the Holy Spirit had been wooing me much of my life as I found joy, peace, and comfort in the worship of the Lord. Now as I look back, I see how God was hovering over me at those times, but I really didn't understand that then. I just needed to be in worship whenever I could and however I could make it possible.

Another inward discipline is prayer. I wrote about prayer in Season 2. Prayer was an important framework of my adult life. As I went through the terrible illness and loss of John, my prayer life grew and gave me strength to move forward as a grieving wife, mother, and teacher. My rote prayers of my youth moved into spoken creative prayer using the format ACTS: Adoration, Confession, Thanksgiving, and Supplication.

- **Adoration:** I used the ACTS words as a jumping off point to speak to God as a person rather than the great high vending machine in Heaven. I learned to spend more time adoring God than making a list of concerns and trying to tell God how to be God. I began to see the holiness of God, the creator of the universe. I adored the Lord for being on this earth and sacrificing for our forever. I learned to love God just because He is God and we are not.

- **Confession:** Confession had been a part of our Lutheran and Presbyterian worship service as a written confession that we all spoke together. As I focused on the ACTS prayer format, I began to recognize my sins and confess them, desiring to turn fully from them. Prior to this season, I never thought much about my sins, but I was more aware of others' sins, scoffing at them. Meanwhile, I had a huge log in my eye, preventing me from seeing where I was falling short.

- **Thanksgiving:** Thanksgiving was something we did on the fourth Thursday of November, but rarely did I think to thank God for the goodness of life regularly. Unfortunately, I lived life taking everything for granted unless I had a concern; then I would ask God to take care of it. As I focused on ACTS, I realized all of life has things to be thankful about even in the very difficult times. I learned to thank God in the midst of the drama because He was there and knew how to transition it for the good of the Kingdom.

- **Supplication:** As I grew in the above three areas of prayer, I learned how to pray for my concerns and for others with God's eyes and heart. My former grocery list of requests turned into seeking for more of God in the lives of others and my own life that we might see what God was saying or doing regarding each situation.

Here are Foster's twelve categories of Spiritual Discipline, and scriptures to help you begin to explore each of them according to the Bible. You might want to choose just one, explore it more, and try to incorporate it into your daily life for three to six months. Once you have incorporated it as part of your life, try another one. Remember, it should give you joy as you come closer to the Lord in incorporating discipline into your spiritual life.

Spiritual Disciplines According to Richard Foster

Inward:

- Meditate: Psalm 119:9-12, Colossians 3:16, Joshua 1:8
- Fasting: Matthew 6:16-18
- Prayer: Matthew 6:5-15
- Study: Psalm 119:17-24

Outward:

- Simplicity: Matthew 6:19-33
- Solitude: 1 Kings 19:11-13
- Submission: Philippians 4:10-13
- Service: Matthew 25:14-30

Corporate:

- Confession: James 5:16
- Worship: Psalm 100
- Guidance: Isaiah 30:21
- Celebration (Fellowship) 1 Corinthians 5:8

Reflection Time

Which of the above disciplines do you have as a part of your life? How does it feel to have those as a part of your Christian life?

_____
_____
_____

Which ones not in your life are you willing to incorporate in the next year? How will you do this?

_____
_____
_____

Look through the Bible to see what God's Word says about each of these Spiritual Disciplines.

Prayer Time

Ask God to help you develop a Spiritually Disciplined life. Ask Him to help you have joy as you add new disciplines to your way of life. Rejoice in the ones you love and have incorporated so far. Each discipline will help you know the Lord more closely. Ask for help in this journey.

Chapter 13
Rooftop-Prayer as a Way of Life

> *"And when you pray, you must not be like the hypocrites. For they love to stand and pray in the synagogues and at the street corners, that they may be seen by others. Truly, I say to you, they have received their reward. But when you pray, go into your room and shut the door and pray to your Father who is in secret. And your Father who sees in secret will reward you."*
>
> — Matthew 6:5-6

Over time, prayer truly became a way of life, from the rote prayers of childhood to a prayer book and worship prayer, into prayer to communicate with God. I learned that prayer should be a conversation with God, rather than just reading a list of concerns. I learned to pray to be shown the will of God and align with what God is doing. This chapter shows you some of the ways I expanded my prayer life.

Pray for an Hour a Day

> *"If my people, who are called by my name, will humble themselves and pray and seek my face and turn from their wicked ways, then I will hear from heaven, and I will forgive their sin and will heal their land."*
>
> — 2 Chronicles 7:14

Over time, prayer became a way of life for me. When I was young, rote and liturgical prayers were all I knew. As a struggling wife, I learned to pray more personal, creative prayers. I prayed each morning, every evening, and at church. Occasionally, I attended a prayer meeting at church and was learning to compose prayers on the spot. But one day, our Christian education director invited me to attend a conference for Christian educators, and my prayer life took a huge leap.

I agreed to attend this conference as a participant in the youth middle program. At the event, I bought a ticket for lunch, which included a keynote address by Becky Tirabassi. I had never heard of her, but I thought it would be good to meet others who were attending the event during lunch. I did that, but the highlight of the luncheon was Becky's message. Her intriguing message was filled with God stories and grabbed ahold of me like a vise. In story after story, she talked about concerns, crises, desires, and wishes, and how God had answered her prayers, often at the last minute or in ways she had never expected. I wanted to pray like Becky prayed. I wanted to learn to trust God in the way Becky trusted God. I wanted to know God the way Becky knew God. She was the answer to my prayer, "I want to pray the best way possible, God." God had indeed given me my prayer language by then, but I had so much more to learn about relationship with God and how to make prayer the center of my day.

Becky challenged us to pray for an hour each day. *What?* I thought. I was a recent widow, mother of three, a fourth-grade teacher, and the manager of our home. How could I ever find an hour a day to pray?

The challenge hit me smack between the eyes. I had to find a way. Becky suggested we begin with a commitment to pray for fifteen minutes each day for a week or two, then add fifteen minutes in a week or so until we reached sixty minutes of prayer. I hadn't let go of the hour of reading in the evening before sleep. That was important to me and my growth, so prayer would have to be in the morning.

I purchased Becky's books *Let Prayer Change Your Life* and *My Partner Prayer Notebook*. The book spoke about prayer and the notebook was an important tool to help me pray longer. Frankly, when I thought about praying for an hour a day, I couldn't imagine what to say for a whole hour. The notebook had sections where Old Testament scripture to pray could be written, then New Testament places to thank God, adore God, and prayer concerns. My prayer time grew slowly to an hour as I prayed over the scripture, joys, and concerns listed in my notebook. As requests were answered, I could praise God and document the response in my notebook.

As I grew in prayer, I began to see the value of praying at lunch time at work. I walked and prayed for a half hour instead of socializing in the teacher's lounge. I prayed as I drove, praying for people who had broken down or for help with directions. I prayed for my children, their education, their friends, my neighbors, my students, my pastors, my future, my struggles, and more and more and more. Life began to be a prayer, which led to a daily journey with the Lord talking to Him as if He were in everything throughout the day. Actually, He always was. I just began to see more of Him and His ways.

I am so grateful for Becky Tirabassi, for our Christian education director who directed me toward the conference, and for Pastor Phil, who encouraged my prayer journey and intimacy with the Lord.

Mountaintop Experiences

> *"About eight days after Jesus said this, He took Peter, John, and James with Him and went on to a mountain to pray. As He was praying, the appearance of His face changed, and His clothes became as bright as a flash of lightning."*
>
> — Luke 9:28-29

During seminary, a time in my life of worship and prayer, I added intentional isolation to allow undisturbed time for prayer, which I called my "Prayer Mountain" times. Prayer mountain time was two or three hours of prayer every Tuesday morning once my daughters were off to school. I tried not to schedule classes during the day on Tuesday because my prayer mountains were so important to me.

I hugged my daughters goodbye and headed back to bed to cover my head and get into a "Prayer Closet" setting. I began by praising God and seeking Him. Then I thanked Him for who He was and what He was becoming to me. I did not pray for others during my prayer mountain times, but just used them to have "mountaintop time" with God. Every Tuesday, He met me there, teaching me, encouraging me, and healing me. I surrendered to His agenda and His plan for the day. These precious times drew me into a deep personal relationship with God, transforming and renewing my life, and bringing clarity.

Once I was in parish ministry, I was unable to carve out a Tuesday morning each week since I was a solo pastor or the director of a ministry. But I did make it part of my call papers to have a day and a half once a month to go away alone with the Lord as an important part of my ministry hours. Once a month, I would leave from Sunday worship and return Tuesday morning ready for work in my office. The leaders in my congregation looked for places for me to retreat to for free as they saw the benefit in my life and ministry. I stayed at church campgrounds during the off seasons when there were no students. I camped in my two-person tent on occasion. A friend of mine owned a cabin in Lake Arrowhead and allowed me to stay there a few times. One church member owned a radio station and gave me motel passes he had received from vendors. It was important for me personally to get away, and it was important for the church for me to spend this time alone with the Lord. Sometimes leaders would say, "I can tell it is time for you to have your spiritual retreat again." And it was indeed. Those precious times helped me in difficult ministry and in my growth as a pastor.

I must say, though, spiritual retreats or mountaintop times are not just for seminary students or pastors. I believe all pastors and seminary students should regularly find ways to be alone with the Lord for a day. Yet I believe that everyone, every Christ follower, needs to learn the value of having time alone with the Lord nurturing their relationship. Every moment will benefit you more than you could ever imagine.

Mountaintop experiences, retreats, and lengthy prayer fall into inward and outward disciplines. These types of intentional prayer getaways help us meditate, pray, fast, find solitude, submit, worship, and even celebrate. Participating in any of these disciplines over a day or two transforms our lives and can direct our path toward the solutions we are seeking.

My Challenge for You

"Do not be anxious about anything, but in everything by prayer and supplication with thanksgiving let your requests be made known to God."
— Philippians 4:6

Just as Becky Tirabassi challenged us to pray for an hour every day, I challenge you to seek the Lord for a longer period at least once a month. In this way, you become sensitive to God's voice and see His direction. In such times, we begin to see our broken areas and how God is anxious to heal them. And it is a time of deep rest as we pray and fall asleep in the Lord's arms, awaking with answers to concerns or revelations that bubble out because we had nothing else on our minds.

I personally believe God desires more of us, and the best way to surrender to God's desire is to begin practicing spiritual disciplines one at a time. Maybe it is consistently worshiping every Sunday. Maybe it is adding fifteen minutes of prayer a day until you are able to pray joyfully for an hour. Maybe it is exploring meditating on God's Word, singing praise songs in the car on the way to and from work, or reading a book about prayer, spiritual disciplines, or the character of God. Maybe it is seriously taking a Bible class, doing the homework, and incorporating what you learn into your life. Whatever you choose, I know for a fact it will enhance your journey with the Lord.

Reflection Time

What is your prayer life like? Do you pray every day, throughout the day?

_____
_____
_____

Try to think about praying constantly. You may need to begin with a commitment to pray for fifteen minutes every day, pray before meals, pray in the morning, and pray before bedtime to begin with.

_____
_____
_____

Have you made prayer part of the rhythm of your life with God? If not, why not? Are you willing to make it so?

_____
_____
_____

Prayer Time

Ask for God's help in planning your day with prayer or more prayer. Ask Him to show Himself to you throughout your day. Ask Him to lead you to a tool that will increase your prayer life, such as a book, journal, or prayer notebook.

Chapter 14

Rooftop-Surrender as a Way of Life

"And as He said to the Father when the time came to surrender His life, 'not my will, but yours be done.'"

— Luke 22:42

In the Foundation season of my life, I took you on a journey of falling in love the world's way. I believe God was in the match between John and me more than I realized in my early twenties. I was so innocent then in my ways. My family foundation of worship, prayer, and discipline was intertwined with the Lord's presence in ways I never understood. Even though John had not grown up in a church-going family, he was hungry for a church family. I am not sure he knew that when we met, but it was natural for us to attend church as one of our first dates. It was natural for us to commit to worshiping together and to praying before we ate as I had done growing up.

Even though God was in the melding of our lives together, we—and later I—had so much more to learn about God and godly ways of life. Worshiping and serving in the church were natural for us, yet much of what we heard was not sinking into our hearts as it should have. We were believers who lived way too much as the world lives. Little by little, the transition happened during John's final few years as I read in the evening and encouraged prayer time before going to sleep at night. We grew, the Spirit became more and more apparent, and God's presence covered us in our times of trial.

In the years after John's death, I was led to replace more of my ways with God's ways. It was truly my hour of prayer, my mountaintop experiences, my inner healing sessions, attending workshops and conferences, and finding new friends that facilitated my slow surrender. I knew I was changing the ways I encountered life's challenges and the ways I thought about others.

I saw the turmoil within me was unwinding. In 1996, the movie *Twister* was in the theaters. It was about scientists studying tornadoes. Each year, the characters in the film anxiously awaited tornado season in the Midwest and "chased" them to study them in hopes of providing quicker warnings. In the movie, the director took us into the center of a tornado through cinemicrography. Suddenly, we were in the eye of the storm where it is silent. Just outside of the eye, we saw cows, trucks, houses, and other debris swirling around. If we reached out of the eye of the storm, we would have been sucked into the chaos of the winds. If we stood still in the silence, we were safe as life swirled all around us.

As I watched the movie, I saw it reflected how life is when we are in the storms all around us, but for us, the eye is God's presence. Once I saw *Twister*, I more fervently sought God's presence in all of the storms of my life. To do that, I had to surrender more and more to God's ways, God's Word, and the Spirit's guidance.

The Castle in My Home

> *"Whoever dwells in the shelter of the Most High will rest in the shadow of the Almighty. I will say of the Lord, 'He is my refuge and my fortress (castle), my God, in whom I trust.'"*
>
> — Psalm 91:1-2

One example of seeking the eye of the storm was during the early days of the COVID-19 pandemic in 2020. I lived in a mobile home park for seniors in the northeast foothills of the Fresno, California, area.

CHAPTER 14: ROOFTOP—SURRENDER AS A WAY OF LIFE

Having to stay in our mobile homes alone made us feel overwhelmingly isolated. My family lived five hours away. We talked occasionally, but frankly it was very lonely. I could not worship with others and only spoke briefly to neighbors across the street.

My solution in this critical time was to seek the eye of this storm as I had when seeking mountaintop experiences in the past. I spent hours and hours with the Lord in my bedroom. He spoke to me often in dreams and visions. In one of the visions, I saw a castle up the road from me. I decided to walk to the castle doors, which had no doorknobs. Wanting to enter into this gigantic place, I decided to sing the song "Majesty." Slowly, the doors opened as I sang, and I bowed down. The presence of the Lord was so powerful I was not able to enter the castle that first day. The next day, I walked up to the castle and sang again. Immediately, the doors slowly opened. This time, I stepped in one step and fell on my knees, then lay on the floor in front of the doors. After a while, I left, and the doors closed. Day after day, I approached the door, sang, the door opened, I walked in a little more each day, knelt, and lay flat in reverence and awe of the overwhelming presence of the Lord inside the castle.

After leaving the castle each day, I saw things in my heart or thoughts that were not fitting for a Christ follower. I surrendered those ways and repented. Each time I approached the castle, I was lighter, and the door opened more quickly. One day, I sang, the doors opened, and in the middle of the room was Jesus sitting in a chair. He signaled for me to come forward. I walked slowly, then knelt at his feet and wept. He reached down and patted my head. I felt peace. Then I left.

Day after day, I processed my life, my brokenness, and my sinful ways as they were revealed. Every day, I surrendered more and more and was forgiven. One day as I sat in my living room on my large, leather chair reading, I glanced at the vase sitting on my kitchen table. My friend had brought me a dozen red roses when she brought me some food and other essential items early in the lockdown. The roses had been in that vase a couple of weeks by then, and they were still red and the leaves were still bright green! That was amazing to me since roses normally last a week or less. I was surprised at their continued beauty but attributed it to the time of year. It was March and cooler in the room where they were placed. I had a fire built in the house to keep me warm, but the dining area was far from the fireplace. What a joy it was to have these beautiful red roses last longer than usual. Yet, I was puzzled by the length of time they bloomed. In the end, I realized it had to be the presence of God resting in my home, the overflow from my daily visits of the spirit-filled castle positively impacting the life of these beautiful cut roses and me.

One afternoon after I went to the castle, prayed, and read, I looked over at the roses and saw something new sticking out of the vase. Whatever it was had not been there before. I walked across the room and saw it was new growth! The stems of the roses were producing new leaves! Day-by-day, more and more little leaves grew from those roses. Those roses remained fresh, red, and growing a month in my vase!

I began to realize the presence of the Lord was very heavy in my home as I approached the castle each day, sang "Majesty," and entered the meeting room. God was not only sustaining those flowers, but He was growing them. Each time I entered the castle, the chair was in the center of the room and Jesus was waiting for me. After several days, another chair appeared, and Jesus offered me a seat so He could wrap His arms around me and hold me. We didn't talk, but His presence was wonderful. I left with more peace, joy, and love. I also felt more freedom from my sins, actions, and ways that were revealed and released.

God's Directives in Preparation

> *"I will instruct you and teach you in the way you should go; I will counsel you with my eye upon you."*
>
> — Psalm 32:8

CHAPTER 14: ROOFTOP—SURRENDER AS A WAY OF LIFE

My castle journey lasted about a month. Then one day, the castle didn't appear and the new growth on the roses began to dwindle. I had exchanged many of my sinful ways for Christ's love and forgiveness. As the castle journey ended, my assignment was to work on restoring the outside of my home. The Lord directed the work I did in my yard. I had purchased a fixer-upper house five years earlier, but I hadn't had time to work in the yard as I had wanted. Now was the time. I removed piles of red decorative stones from the soil. A friend called it terraplaning the land. I was certainly doing that. Every stone I removed indicated a sin, brokenness, or negative thought that God had been removing while inside. As I removed the red stones, I boxed them for further use. I was to trim bushes and the lower parts of trees. I cut away the excess branches and dead pieces as a recognition of the excess and dead things that were pruned from my life.

Then came the process of sanding and patching the wooden shed, which had never been painted. Day after day, I did all of this work alone with the guidance of the Lord until it was time to paint my shed. I was not able to climb the ladder to paint the top half of the shed. God provided a godly friend to paint the top half for me. The work on the shed was a reminder that God was restoring my life as He and I did this outside renovation project, and He brings help as we need assistance in life.

Previous owners had used scalloped cement edging around the flowerbed, but they had been tipped over or covered in dirt. I dug them all out and stacked them until it was time to replace them in the proper places around my yard. I pulled bags of weeds and dug out a huge, dead bush. Then came my wooden deck. Once again, I pulled out my trusty sander and got to work. The wood was old and needed a lot of patching and sealing, and finally, I painted it with two coats of deck paint.

I repaired my side fence and rebuilt a small fence between the deck and the fence. I painted all of the fencing alongside my home, and I trimmed back the six-foot tall bushes alongside each side of my home.

The steps in the back of my house were in terrible condition. I repaired a large piece of wood that was not safe, then sanded it, painted it, and installed moldings on the steps and around the railing. The final project the Lord instructed me to do was the skirting around my house. He wanted me to remove all of the pieces, clean them, straighten the misshaped pieces, and reinstall them.

Daily, I prayed as I did the work He instructed. The edging was to place a spiritual edging of protection around my property. The deck and the back steps were to protect and bless all who would enter this home. The repairs of the wooden shed were to protect all of the outside tools from the hands of intruders. The removal of the red stones and weeds were to remove all of the dark spirits that had lingered around this home for many years.

Once the roses had died and the castle came no more, the assignment outside was to bring the spiritual presence around the outside of my home. That process took a year and a half of my own work. It was all during COVID-19 lockdown, and I had the time and the tools. I also knew my hands were the hands to complete this work. The only help was painting my shed, and a neighbor helped me paint the top of my wooden fence.

My New Era of Life

> *"Therefore, if anyone is in Christ, the new creation has come: the old has gone, the new is here!"*
>
> — 2 Corinthians 5:17

I had known for some time that I was to prepare my home to sell since I had retired from parish ministry nine months prior to COVID

CHAPTER 14: ROOFTOP—SURRENDER AS A WAY OF LIFE

lockdown. I had desired to move closer to my family in Southern California. Every time I completed a project outside, I felt like my home was ready to sell. And every time, He directed me to complete another project and pray as I completed the work. The ground was tilled; the edging was like the spiritual wall around the property. Dead branches and bushes were the removal of my sins that had taken place in this house over the many years. The skirting was the protection of the home's foundation, as was the repair and painting of the deck and back steps. Every project had a spiritual meaning for me and for the home.

I lived in a two-year period of complete surrender and growth in the Lord. One day, I awoke hearing, "Phoenix." I immediately spoke out loud, "What does that mean, Lord? I don't want to live in the desert again. Oh well, if that is what you want, okay." In that brief statement, my heart moved from negativity to joy. Obedience to the Lord was the only option I could have.

Soon, I began to search online for senior independent apartments. Since my youngest daughter lived in the Phoenix area, I asked her to check out locations for me. Phoenix has hundreds of senior housing locations since many seniors travel to the area during the winter or to retire. It seemed like an overwhelming task to find the right place to live. A few days later, I heard, "It is like a needle in a haystack. I want you to focus on Mesa." Wow! That narrowed down the search considerably for me.

Since I was to visit my daughter at the beginning of November 2021, I made a list of locations to check out. One was at the top of my list because I had spoken to the executive director, Jeramy, a couple of times and the online pictures were wonderful.

On November 1, I visited the apartment complex and really liked what I saw, but I had to have my daughter agree on this location with me. I visited, on a Monday. On Tuesday, Jeramy informed me that a tenant had turned in her notice for a two-bedroom apartment in the model where I was interested in living. I could have it if I wanted it. Wednesday, my daughter and I returned to the complex and were able to tour the apartment, which would be open as of December 31, 2021.

I loved that the apartment was on the north side, away from the blazing summer heat, plus the complex had many other amenities.

My season of visiting the castle, the work in the yard, and my new home were all a part of my surrendered life that was about to end. After placing a deposit on the "chosen apartment," I returned for the final outside touches on my home and began to pack. I rented a local storage unit for an end-of-the-year cheap rate, and with the help of my precious neighbor Jane, I began the process of storing what I would move to Arizona and donating what would not move with me.

By the time I had all of the house repairs completed and many things packed, the Lord informed me it was time to sell my home. "Lord, it is now close to Christmas; who will be looking to buy a home in this cold, damp, Christmas season? Well, *you* will have to sell it!" Within two days, a woman from my congregation who had moved to Canada had returned to the area. We had remained Facebook friends, and she had watched the process of the outside preparations of my home. One morning, she messaged me that she was interested in looking at my home. That morning, she offered to buy it with cash! Within days of my trip to Southern California for family Christmas, God had sold my home. She was not worried about the exact move in date, allowing me time for family and a return to finish packing, handling official paperwork with the state, and arranging a moving company. God had provided a buyer a week before Christmas and picked out my new apartment in a new state, with little effort on my part!

As I reflect on that period of time, I think about how God sent Abraham to a new land that was not of Abraham's choosing, and how he lifted the Israelites out of Egypt and led them through the wilderness to the

Promised land. Each of their journeys were times of surrender to the Lord for His ways, not theirs. Life was good when they obeyed, and a challenge when they chose their ways. I continue to seek the eye of the storm in my new life in my new territory, Mesa, Arizona. I continue to discover ways and thoughts that are not pleasing to the Lord, and I SURRENDER them to Him as I reach up to Him for His plan or His ways.

My apartment is my sanctuary, which I now share with my sweet little Yorkie, Sophia. She was brought to me by the Lord because she needed a home and I needed a companion. She needed love, and I needed to have someone to love. God knows our needs often when we don't even realize what we need.

My Hope for You

> *"You were taught, with regard to your former way of life, to put off your old self, which is being corrupted by its deceitful desire; to be made new in the attitude of your minds; and to put on the new self, created to be like God in true righteousness and holiness."*
>
> — Ephesians 4:22-24

Life is an adventure. I have chosen to make that adventure with the King who has a plan for me and for each of us. He is the King of Kings and Lord of Lords. He has sent His Spirit to live within us, leading us, challenging us, convicting us, and loving us. It is the Spirit who illuminates our broken ways so that the Healer, Lord Jesus, is able to heal us and transform our hearts.

My heart is definitely not as it was when I landed on this earth, nor at the time of the loss of John. The evolution of my life rapidly transformed as I opened the door of my heart wide for Jesus to have His way. This journey will continue to evolve until I am permanently in the Kingdom of Heaven.

My prayer is that this book gives you hope for your future. I pray it challenges you to go on a deeper journey into your soul with the One who is truly safe and loves you more than life itself. Blessings as you seek Him.

Reflection Time

Is your life clearly in the hands and will of the Lord? Take some time to think about this question and write why you say what you say.

_____

_____

_____

If not, are you willing to let go and let Him lead, guide, and heal your life, directing your path every inch of the way? You might want to pray something like this, "Lord, this is all new to me, but I want more of you. Open my heart, my soul, and my mind to more of you in my life." Write about what you said to God, and how you might move forward.

_____

_____

_____

Are you stuck in a place and don't know in which direction to move? Ask and listen, and He will lead the way. Just be willing to go where He directs.

_____

_____

_____

Prayer Time

Lord, thank you that you care about every aspect of our lives, our hearts, our minds, our souls, and our ways. Bless the readers; lead them as you have led me. I pray that you continue to show each of us your ways. In Christ's name. Amen.

Epilogue

"Our Father in heaven, hallowed be your name, your kingdom come, your will be done, on earth as it is in heaven."
— Matthew 6:9-10

Thy Kingdom Come

In Chapter 6, I wrote about the prayers I learned as a child, which included the Lord's Prayer. I must say that knowing and repeating the prayer the Lord taught us to pray unified me with others. At bedtime, my family spoke the words together as we prepared for bed. On Sunday, all the adults and the pastor spoke the same words I learned at home. I felt like an important person in our church because I could say this prayer just like all of the adults. I didn't understand much of the meaning as a five-year-old, but I could say the prayer. Over the years, I spoke those words at least 14,000 times as I prayed the Lord's Prayer every day and sometimes twice on Sunday. It was a sacred prayer to me, but the meaning kind of floated through me with little personal impact.

Then one day when I was attending a Sunday evening prayer group at our church in Vacaville, California, one of the pastors suggested we close with the Lord's Prayer. *Okay*, I thought, *that will put the rubber stamp of goodness on our evening of prayer.* But as I spoke the words, they became more alive for me, especially the words, "Thy Kingdom come, thy will be done on earth as it is in Heaven." Wow! I suddenly had an *aha* moment that forever changed my life. As I drove home, I spoke to the Lord saying, "Lord, your prayer says, 'Thy Kingdom come, thy will be done on earth as it is in Heaven.' What does that look like? What is the Kingdom on earth? How can we live in thy will on earth just like in Heaven?"

The more I thought about the Kingdom on Earth, the more I recognized a kingdom has to have a King, and that is King Jesus. He is my Brother, and He is my King. If He is my King, then I am also the Father's daughter. The daughter of the King has certain rights and expectations that others don't have. What are those rights and expectations? How do I go about living as the daughter of the Lord? I asked, and asked, prayed, and listened as God began to bring people into my life to teach me, even though they didn't really understand they were specifically teaching me to live as Papa God's daughter.

During the last few weeks before I headed off to college, I went to Utica, Michigan, to visit my grandparents (my dad's parents). I was excited to tell them I would be taking German in my first quarter to better understand their mother tongue. My year of high school German had exposed me to the written language and basic communication, but I hoped to write and communicate better with my grandparents in the language they loved. I promised I would write some letters to them from college.

When it was time for me to head home, I hugged each of them, and Grandpa said, "Don't do anything that would embarrass the family." Now that was surprising to me because Grandpa had pulled many shenanigans in his life, and in this case, he was like the pot calling the kettle black. I was a good girl and had always been good. I had never done anything that would embarrass the family. Yet his statement put a certain expectation on me as I headed out on my new adventure away from home. This exciting adventure would begin with the reminder to remain aligned with the teachings and ways of the Meyer family. I was a Meyer through and through, and I had to remember that as I stepped into the world.

Fast forward to my discovery of the Kingdom here on the Earth. I could understand that just as Grandpa had placed expectations on my college years, so, too, God places expectations on our lives. Those expectations are meant to keep us aligned with God's dreams and plans for our lives, which are achieved by lining up our actions and words with God's teachings and desires for us. God does not have us on a string, controlling our every move. We have free will, yet, in our freedom, we need to choose to live according to God's desires as revealed in His Word. This alignment keeps us safe and in the goodness of relationship with God.

The more I explored God's principles, the more I realized where there is "love, honor, and respect," the peace, joy, and order of the Lord can spill out of us, drawing others into the Kingdom, which includes the grace of God and celebration.

During my ministry with military wives in San Diego County, our ministry leader often quoted, "Love your neighbor as yourself." Now this ministry was expansive, ranging all through the 4,200 square miles, including massive Camp Pendleton, Camp Miramar, Naval Base Point Loma, Naval Base Coronado, and others. We worked with the spouses of enlisted personnel, and most had children. It seemed there was never enough money for most of them for food, diapers, formula, and even clothing/furnishings. The director used this piece of scripture in a way that caused us to rush around with mercy in our hearts to meet all of the needs of many of these women. It was costly to all of us on staff, as it was in the director's own life. As staff, we were expected to be ready at a moment's notice to come to the aid of a young military spouse.

One evening, I was pondering this piece of scripture and decided to look it up in my New International Version (NIV) Bible to find the entire passage. Mark 12:28-31:

> One of the teachers of the law came and heard them debating. Noticing that Jesus had given them a good answer, he asked him, "Of all the commandments, which is most important?"
>
> "The most important one," answered Jesus, "is this: 'Hear, O Israel: The Lord our God, the Lord is one. Love the Lord your God with all your heart and with all your soul and with all your mind and with all your strength.' The second is this: 'Love your neighbor as yourself.' There is no commandment greater than these."

Jesus' words command us to love God first and foremost in everything. Then we are to love our neighbor as ourselves. From that reading forward, I worked to align my life with *all* of this piece of scripture. First to love God with everything: all of my heart, all of my soul, all of my mind, and all of my strength. Then love myself, and out of all of that, love my neighbors. As we are in alignment with God and His perfect love, He reveals where and to whom our love actions are to flow.

It was on my roof that I began to understand the truth of this scripture. My love for the Lord exploded as I reached up and allowed His healing hands to touch my brokenness and sinful nature. The more I surrendered to Him, the more He could heal and grow me in His will and His ways. My life transferred to an intimate life with Him daily until the presence took over and I experienced the life of Being a Living Sanctuary.

Your journey may be nothing like my journey; nonetheless, your journey can be deeper and higher than you know is possible. He can take you deeper into your soul with the Spirit's light to reveal what is hidden or needs healing. By the grace of the Healer, Jesus, we can become more aligned with King Jesus and His plan for our lives. As we reach up, He can take us to higher places of intimacy, revealing new truths, peace, and joy that comes with Kingdom Life on the earth with King Jesus.

Blessings and grace to you, Beloved Daughters and Sons of our Lord. Enjoy your journey!

"Thy Kingdom come on the Earth as it is in Heaven."

Now What?

Wrapping It Up

I have taken you on a journey through three seasons of my life to help you explore the seasons of your life. Season 1 was the Foundations of my life, placed there mostly by my parents as they lived out their foundational pieces. It was exciting for me to discover in the writing of my story the solid foundations I began life standing upon.

Season 2 was the Framework that John and I built around our family, which was strong and able to hold us up when we encountered the greatest crisis of our lives—his illness and death. My and my children's grieving period was supported by the Framework of our lives: family and personal friends, church family, financial security, and prayer. Without any one of these walls in our home, we would have been floundering even more than we were. I thank God for helping us build these walls to make us strong.

Season 3 was the building of the roof upon the solid Framework. The roof tiles were: Hearing God, Experiencing God, Heart Healing, Spiritual Disciplines, Intimate Prayer. Each of these tiles transformed my home into a Living Sanctuary, a Sanctuary that surrounds me and lives within me. Within this Sanctuary, the Father (Papa God), the Son, and the Holy Spirit have an active part in my life every day. The process of healing, leading, guiding, challenging, growing, and loving continues as I notice the active work of the Triune God in the Purpose and Plans of my life.

My journey has been a seventy-plus-year journey from the rote prayers and worship of my youth to the castle and outside preparation of my home. All were a major part of building my personal sanctuary where the Lord resides. I started this journey in a committed Christian family and accepted the family faith in Jesus as mine. The last season was a unique journey with no one holding my hand except God. No one led the way. No one said, "Come this way." I merely followed the Lord's lead. I took every opportunity to learn, grow, and discover more about God.

Now It Is Your Turn!

I hope you completed the reflections throughout this book to help you explore your Foundation, Framework, and Roof. If you haven't, I suggest you go back to the beginning, ponder the questions, and pray the suggested prayers or prayers of your own.

If you need assistance in developing your own Foundation, Framework, and Roof, here are a few additional tools:

- I also have a companion workbook/journal with scripture, more stories, and opportunities for you to go deeper within yourself. As you search your inner thoughts, explore your wounds, and release them to the Lord, you will begin to find victory for your life and more room for Jesus to live within you, as you become His Sanctuary. The workbook/journal will be called *Becoming a Living Sanctuary Workbook* and be available on Amazon in summer 2023.

- Message me on Messenger (Sandy Meyer Bowen) to set up Inner Healing or Clarity Call sessions.

- Find me on Facebook: Joyful Kingdom Living, Alive in Christ, Alive in the Spirit, or Loving as Jesus Commanded. I offer classes and challenges regularly. You can find the most recent ones on this Facebook site.
- Books, classes, inner healing, clarity calls, and other info may be found on my Facebook site, Sandy Meyer Bowen-Author.

Thank you for going on this journey with me!

Blessings and grace,

Sandy Meyer Bowen

Sandy Meyer Bowen

Author, Speaker, Teacher, Mentor, Inner Healing Minister, Retired Public Educator, Retired Pastor, and Founder of Joyful Kingdom Living

Bibliography

Book References

Anderson, Neil T. *The Bondage Breaker.* Eugene, OR: Harvest House Publishing, 2006.

-------. *Steps to Freedom in Christ.* Raleigh, NC: Regal Books, 2000.

-------. *Victory Over Darkness.* Cleveland, OH: Great Lakes Publishing, 1991.

Brother Lawrence. *The Practice of the Presence of God.* Washington, DC: ICS Publication, 1984.

Chapman, Gary. *The Five Love Languages.* Bhopai, Madhya Pradesh, India: Manjul Publishing House, 2001.

Foster, Richard. *The Celebration of Disciplines.* Hachette, UK: Hodder & Stoughton Publishing, 2008.

Tirabassi, Becky. *Letting Prayer Change Your Life.* Nashville, TN: Thomas Nelson, 1995.

Ministry References

Cleansing Stream, PO Box 3765, Antioch, CA 04531-3765, www.cleansingstream.org

Lutheran Renewal Ministries. www.lutheranrenewal.org. Paul Anderson, Director.

Presbyterian Reformed Ministries International, PO Box 429, Black Mountain, NC 28711-0429, prmi@prmi.org. Brad Long and Cindy Strickler, Executive Directors.

Music

"Beautiful Savior." Source Gesangbuch, Munster, 1677. English translator Joseph Augustus Seiss, 1842. Public domain.

"I Love You, Lord." Laurie Klein. Vocalists Maranatha Singers. 1978.

"Lord, I Lift Your Name on High." Rick Founds. Vocalists Maranatha Singers. 1989.

Family Rote Prayers—Our Foundation of Prayer
(Fold your hands!)

Bedtime

- **Our first bedtime prayer**

Now I lay me down to sleep
I pray the Lord my soul to keep,
If I should die before I wake,
I pray the Lord my soul to take.

- **Added once we were a little older, about age five**

Our Father who art in heaven
Hallowed be thy name
Thy Kingdom come
Thy will be done on earth as it is in heaven
Give us this day our daily bread
And forgive our debts
As we forgive our debtors
And lead us not into temptation

But deliver us from evil
For thine is the Kingdom
And the power and the glory
Forever.

Amen.

Mealtime

- **Our very first prayer we learned as soon as we could talk in short sentences.**

Abba, liebe, Vater. Amen.
(meaning - Daddy, love, Father. So be it.)

- **Before eating**

Come Lord Jesus,
Be our guest,
Let these thy gifts to us be blessed.

- **After eating**

Oh, give thanks unto the Lord
For He is good
And His mercy endures forever.

About the Author

Sandy Meyer Bowen was born and raised in the suburbs northeast of Detroit, Michigan. In 1993, she and her family moved to Vacaville, California, to live near her mother-in-law, and to enjoy the beauty and history of California, her husband's home state. Sandy has three grown children, two in-law children, and four grandsons. Additionally, her youngest daughter is a foster mom, and she rejoices in being grandma to these foster babies. Sandy graduated from Michigan State University in 1969 with a BA in Elementary Education. She earned an MA in Elementary Education from Saginaw Valley State University in 1979 and a Master of Divinity from Fuller Theological Seminary in Pasadena, California in 1996. This education was important for her two serving careers as an elementary school public educator and an ordained Presbyterian pastor and an ordained Lutheran pastor. At times, her two careers overlapped, but she taught school for twenty-five years and pastored for twenty years in many different locations.

In 1987, Sandy's husband passed away from brain cancer. At the time, the family lived in Vacaville, California, and her children were ages nine, eleven, and thirteen. This family tragedy tremendously impacted Sandy and her children. As devastating as the loss was, Sandy, with the lead of the Holy Spirit, developed a personal relationship with Jesus and the Holy Spirit. This journey became the reason for writing this book, and for helping others to discover their personal identities in Christ and His Kingdom purpose for their lives.

Sandy moved from the location of her final parish ministry, Auberry, California, to Mesa, Arizona, in January, 2022. She lives near her youngest daughter and regularly visits her son and family in Huntington Beach. Her older daughter and family are missionaries in El Salvador, where Sandy has visited several times.

Sandy now uses her teaching, mentoring, writing, and speaking gifts to help others grow deeper in their relationship with the Lord through her movement, Joyful Kingdom Living. She does this by offering online classes, speaking engagements, inner healing, and book and journal writing.

Connect with Sandy

Here are ways to connect with Sandy for further information:

Facebook:

- Sandy Meyer Bowen
- Becoming a Living Sanctuary
- Alive in Christ
- Messenger

Instagram: @sandymeyerbowen
Website: www.BecomingALivingSanctuary.com
Email: joyfulkingdomliving@gmail.com

Becoming a Living Sanctuary Devotional Journal to be released in mid-2023.

Classes being offered through Zoom:

- Reflection and Devotional class using *Secrets of the Vine* by Bruce Wilkerson
- Alive in Christ
- Sending the Spirit—a course on Pentecost
- Becoming a Living Sanctuary Study-Deep Dive
- All courses are live and saved in Facebook groups for class members

Made in the USA
Columbia, SC
21 February 2023